Israel Horovitz's

UNEXPECTED TENDERNESS

SAMUEL FRENCH, INC.

45 West 25th Street   NEW YORK 10010
7623 Sunset Boulevard HOLLYWOOD 90046
LONDON   TORONTO

IMPORTANT BILLING AND CREDIT REQUIREMENTS

All producers of Israel Horovitz's Unexpected Tenderness *must* give credit to the Author of the Play in all programs distributed in connection with performances of the Play and in all instances in which the title of the Play appears for purposes of advertising, publicizing or otherwise exploiting the Play and/or a production. The name of the Author *must* also appear on a separate line, on which no other name appears, immediately **above the title**, and *must* appear in size of type not less than fifty percent the size of the title type.

In addition, the following credit must appear in all programs and publications used in connection with a production and/or advertising, publicizing or otherwise exploiting a production:

Israel Horovitz's "Unexpected Tenderness" was given its world premiere at the Gloucester Stage Company (Israel Horovitz, Artistic Director) and its subsequent New York City premiere in 1994 at the WPA Theatre (Kyle Renick, Artistic Director).

Unexpected Tenderness had its world premiere at the Gloucester Stage Company in Gloucester, Massachusetts on August 19, 1994. It was directed by Grey Johnson. The set was designed by Charles F. Morgan, the lighting by John Ambrosone, the costumes by Jane Stein. The stage manager was James Conway. Assistant stage manager was Charlotte Vuarnesson. The cast was as follows:

Roddy Stern (the Elder)/Archie Stern ---------------------- Will LeBow

Roddy Stern (the Younger)------------------- Ben Webster, David Rich

Molly Stern---Paula Plum

Sylvie Stern ---Jessica Semeraro

Haddie Stern -- Patricia Pellows

Jacob Stern --Barry Zaslove

Willie--Mick Verga

Unexpected Tenderness subsequently had its New York City premiere was on October 16, 1994 at the WPA Theatre. It was directed by Steve Zuckerman. The set was designed by Edward T. Gianfrancesco, the lighting by Richard Winkler, the costumes by Mimi Maxmen and the sound by Aural Fixation. The production stage manager was Mark Cole. The cast was as follows:

Roddy Stern (the Elder)/Archie Stern ----------------------- Steve Ryan

Roddy Stern (the Younger)-------------------- Jonathan Marc Sherman

Molly Stern-- Caitlin Clarke

Sylvie Stern --- Karen Goberman

Haddie Stern --Scotty Bloch

Jacob Stern --Sol Frieder

Willie-- Paul O'Brien

For My Mother

CHARACTERS

ARCHIE STERN, late 30's, handsome, strong, sad-eyed, suspicious. NOTE: Same actor plays RODDY (The Elder) throughout play.

MOLLY STERN, Archie's wife; slightly younger than Archie; small, full-breasted, strikingly beautiful.

SYLVIE STERN, Archie and Molly's daughter; 15, skinny, sad-eyed, pretty.

RODDY (The Younger) STERN, Archie and Molly's son; 14, small, skinny, an easy smile. (NOTE: Could be played by slightly older actor, age 20-25.)

HADDIE STERN, Archie's mother; nearly 70; small, strong-backed, plump.

JACOB STERN, Archie's father; same age as Haddie; has severe Parkinson's Disease; slurred speech; cannot walk unassisted.

WILLIE, Archie's helper, 40; vaguely dapper.

TIME & PLACE

Early 1950's; Eisenhower is in.
Kitchen of Stern family home, small town New England.

NOTE: If possible, a North Shore Massachusetts accent ("Pahk Yo'r Cah In Hav'id Yahd") should be used by all, but for Haddie and Jacob, who should speak with a accent that is a blend of Eastern Europe and Western Massachusetts.

Mary, Mary,
Quite contrary,
How does your garden grow?

With brittle Shells
And broken Bells,
And one magnificent Fame Lily.

UNEXPECTED TENDERNESS

ACT I

Scene 1

MUSIC IN: Chopin, on piano, lightly, sweetly.

SOFT WHITE LIGHT FADES UP on RODDY (THE ELDER) STERN, center stage. HE is in his late thirties; wears clothing of a truck-driver ... matching grey "chino" pants and shirt, work boots, etc. HE is handsome, sturdy, strong.

A SECOND SPOTLIGHT fades up on RODDY (THE YOUNGER), standing on staircase, facing audience.

RODDY. (THE ELDER) For the past few months, I wake during the night, two or three times, every night, and I hear voices in the kitchen. It's my mother and my father. I hear them bickering, mostly ... But, sometimes, they laugh, and when their laughter stops, I know that they're kissing.

RODDY. (THE YOUNGER) (*Smiles at audience; speaks.*) Each time, just before their voices go silent, they take turns yelling up the stairs for me to get ready for school.

MOLLY'S VOICE. (*Off.*) Roddy! You'll be late for school!

(*RODDY (The ELDER) turns, yells. NOTE: HE is now playing ARCHIE.)*

ARCHIE. Do you hear what your mother's saying, you?

(*HE switches back to playing RODDY (The ELDER), without hesitation ... or explanation to audience.)*

RODDY. (THE ELDER) When I give in to my curiosity and go downstairs, the kitchen's empty, of course, and I'm filled with despair.

MOLLY'S VOICE. (*Off.*) Roddy! You'll be late for school!

(*RODDY (The ELDER) yells upstairs. HE is, again, playing ARCHIE.)*

ARCHIE. It's six-thirty, you! Are you quitting school?! (*No reply.*) Do you hear me? I am asking you a question: Are you quitting school?!

(*ARCHIE turns, faces audience, again; smiles. HE is, now, once again, playing RODDY (The ELDER).)*

RODDY. (THE ELDER) Oh, there's something I should warn you about. I'll be playing Archie, my father—like I just did, there, when I yelled. The boy who's playing Roddy (me, young) will sometimes talk to you, directly, when I'm too busy playing Archie to stop and explain things.

RODDY. (THE YOUNGER) (*Smiles at audience; speaks.*) This confusion of father and son might be a bit disquieting, at first, just like the confusion of father and son is in life. (*Nods to Roddy (The Elder).*) Okay?

RODDY. (THE ELDER) (*Nods "okay"; smiles at audience.*) You're clever. You'll get used to it.

(*Suddenly, RODDY (The YOUNGER) runs upstairs, and RODDY (The ELDER) moves to bottom of staircase, yells upstairs. HE is, once again, playing ARCHIE.*)

ARCHIE. Excuse me! Am I talking to myself here?

(*LIGHTS WIDEN TO REVEAL kitchen, Archie and Molly Stern's modest house. The dining table is set for breakfast. SYLVIE, the daughter, fifteen, sits at upright piano, practicing Chopin etude. SYLVIE is dark-haired, sad-eyed, skinny, pretty. SHE wears a Girl Scout uniform; many merit badges.*
MOLLY enters from outside with milk bottle. SHE is slightly younger than Archie, small, large-breasted, strikingly beautiful; wears robe belted tightly at waist. SHE pour milk, coffee.)

ARCHIE, standing at bottom of staircase, yells upstairs, again.)

ARCHIE. Do you not hear me? I have to be back on the road in one half hour, precisely! ... Willie's waiting in the truck! Do I not deserve to have breakfast with my family? Do you think I'm a stupid person, or what?

(RODDY (The YOUNGER), Archie's fourteen-year-old son, yells down stairs.)

RODDY. (THE YOUNGER) (*Off.*) I'm up! I'm up!
ARCHIE. Yuh, right! So's Mrs. Woolf!
RODDY. (THE YOUNGER) (*Off.*) Who's Mrs. Woolf?
ARCHIE. Your teacher's not Mrs. Woolf?
RODDY. (THE YOUNGER) (*Off.*) My teacher's Mrs. Foxx!
SYLVIE. His teacher's Mrs.. Foxx.
MOLLY. His teacher's Mrs.. Foxx.
The toaster popped! Sylvie! The toaster popped! Are you a *deaf person*?
SYLVIE. (*Stops playing piano.*) Okay, fine, I'm getting it!

(SYLVIE goes to toaster, places toast on plate; goes to stove, begins scrambling eggs. MOLLY gives ARCHIE his coffee.)

MOLLY. (*To Archie.*) Why isn't he up?

ARCHIE. He's up.

MOLLY. How do you know?

ARCHIE. Because, he's talking. He said the words "I'm up," twice. I heard him. If he weren't talking and I didn't hear him, it would be a different story. (*Eyes Molly's robe.*) Close your robe tighter.

MOLLY. (*Tightens belt on robe; yells up stairs to Roddy.*) Are you really up, you?

(*No reply.*)

MOLLY. Roddy!

RODDY. (THE YOUNGER) (*Off.*) I'm really up! I'm really up! I'm practicing my speech for the Red Feather Oratory Contest!

ARCHIE. Now, we both heard him. He's really up. He said he's practicing his Red Feather speech.

MOLLY. (*Returns to kitchen, sets glasses.*) Friday, he said he was practicing his speech for the Red Feather Oratory Contest, and, forty-five minutes later, I went upstairs ... still in bed ...

ARCHIE. You told me ...

MOLLY. ... Sound asleep.

ARCHIE. You told me this.

MOLLY. (*Screams up staircase.*) If you're not downstairs by the time I count twenty-five, there will be no Red Feather Oratory Contest, no bicycle, no skating, no YMCA, and, definitely, no Buzzy Levine! ... One! ... Two! ... (*Takes Archie's empty coffee cup.*) ... Three! ... Four! ... Five! ...

(THEY kiss. MOLLY breaks from kiss; yells upstairs to Roddy.)

MOLLY. *Ten!*

(LIGHTS CROSSFADE with ARCHIE, as HE steps forward into spotlight; talks to audience. MOLLY resumes meal preparation.)

RODDY. (THE ELDER) Oh, I know what you're thinking ... "Sweet, nice little family ... ethnic comedy ... New Englandy ..." ... If I could rewrite it, and make it sweet and nice, I would have done just that ... many years ago!

(Suddenly, RODDY (The ELDER) turns upstage, screams at SYLVIE, who has prepared a breakfast tray. HE is now, again, playing ARCHIE.)

ARCHIE. What do you think you're doing with that?
SYLVIE. Bringing Willie's breakfast out to him.
ARCHIE. (*Enraged. HE moves upstage, to kitchen.*) Jesus! Stop, you! ... Stop!
SYLVIE. Why? I did it yesterday.
ARCHIE. That was yesterday. I ... said ... "Stop!"
SYLVIE. (*Skids to a stop.*) Okay. I stopped.
ARCHIE. (*To Molly.*) Did you see her? Did you see your daughter? Did you see where she was going? (*To*

Sylvie.) If I ever—EVER—see you near *that one*, alone, you'll pack your bags.

SYLVIE. I won't ever, Daddy.

ARCHIE. You're goddam right you won't ever! Gimme that!

(SYLVIE hands breakfast tray to ARCHIE.)

SYLVIE. Here, Daddy.

ARCHIE. Where's his coffee?

SYLVIE. In the thermos bottle. I'll get it.

(MOLLY hands thermos to SYLVIE and SHE hands it to ARCHIE, who tucks it under his arm, carries tray to door.)

ARCHIE. I'll be right back. (*ARCHIE goes to door, stops, turns to Sylvie.*) It's a good thing I asked you, isn't it? (*Exits.*)

SYLVIE. (*After a pause; to the world.*) I never get anything right for him!

MOLLY. Did you finish your Chopin?

SYLVIE. I finished my Chopin.

MOLLY. (*Looks at table.*) No *napkins*? Are we eating like *Irish* people?

SYLVIE. I thought I put napkins on the table. (*SYLVIE gets napkins from sideboard; puts them on table.*)

MOLLY. Did you brush your hair?

SYLVIE. I think I did.

MOLLY. Brush it, again.

SYLVIE. But, I really think I brushed it, already!

MOLLY. Either put a sign on your head that says "I think I brushed it, already," or, go brush it!

SYLVIE. Both of you hate me!

(SYLVIE runs up stairs. MOLLY completes the counting.)

MOLLY. Twenty-two! ... Twenty-three! ... Twenty-four! ...

(RODDY (The YOUNGER) runs down stairs and into room. HE is fourteen years old; dark-eyed, small, skinny.)

RODDY. (THE YOUNGER) *(Radio-announcer's voice.)* And, once again, ladies and gentlemen, Rodney Stern is saved by the click of his Schick!

(MOLLY slaps Roddy's hand, twice.)

MOLLY. This is for your being late, and this is for your Mr. Wiseguy mouth!

RODDY. (THE YOUNGER) Thank you.

(JACOB enters with HADDIE. HE is nearly seventy; has severe Parkinson's Disease. HE walks forward, SHE walks backward. It is almost as if they are dancing. When JACOB talks, his words blur.)

HADDIE. Doesn't he look better?
MOLLY. Much better.
JACOB. I ... d-d-d-don't!
HADDIE. You do!
MOLLY. Say "Hello" to your grandmother.
RODDY. (THE YOUNGER) Hullo, Grandma.
HADDIE. Hello, Roddy. Did you sleep?
RODDY. (THE YOUNGER) I slept.
MOLLY. And not your grandfather?
RODDY. (THE YOUNGER) Hullo, Grandpa.
HADDIE. Doesn't Grandpa look much better?
RODDY. (THE YOUNGER) I guess.
HADDIE. Look at his color.
RODDY. (THE YOUNGER) That's nice, Grandpa.

(HADDIE and JACOB have negotiated a crossing of the kitchen and now attempt to negotiate a seating.)

HADDIE. Chair!
MOLLY. Chair!

(RODDY grabs chair, pulls it back from the table. HADDIE seems to be dumping JACOB onto the floor. At the last possible second, RODDY (The YOUNGER) places the chair under JACOB's bottom, and HE is seated. This is a well-rehearsed, often-performed Stern Family acrobatic act.)

HADDIE. You're comfortable?
JACOB. N-n-no.

HADDIE. Why not? What's to be uncomfortable about? It's your chair! It's your family!

RODDY. (THE YOUNGER) Do you want your cushion, Grandpa?

MOLLY. (*Crosses right to sideboard to check school books.*) Hasn't he got his cushion?

HADDIE. He's got his cushion ... He wants his newspaper ... I'll get your newspaper

(HADDIE exits into front of house; out upstage door. JACOB looks at RODDY (The YOUNGER), furtively.)

JACOB. T-t-take ...

RODDY. (THE YOUNGER) Take your cushion away?

JACOB. Y-y-yes.

(RODDY (The YOUNGER) tries to extricate cushion from under JACOB's bottom, but cannot manage the move.)

RODDY. (THE YOUNGER) Can you kinda hop up a little, Grandpa?

(JACOB tries, but, his hops get him nowhere.)

MOLLY. (*Crosses left from sideboard; en route to table.*) What are you doing to your grandfather, you?

RODDY. (THE YOUNGER) His cushion's bothering him.

MOLLY. Take it out from under him.

RODDY. (THE YOUNGER) I'm trying to.

(ARCHIE appears at window, peeking inside at his family, discreetly, mysteriously. RODDY (The YOUNGER) sees him. After a moment's pause, ARCHIE disappears from window.)

RODDY. (THE YOUNGER) He's coming back inside!

MOLLY. He's coming back inside!

JACOB. He's c-c-c-c ...

MOLLY. *Shhhhh!*

(ARCHIE re-enters from outside.
RODDY helps JACOB with napkin, sugar in his coffee, etc.)

ARCHIE. Willie's sick ... I'll have to take him to the doctor.

MOLLY. What's the matter? *(Cross center to Archie.)*

ARCHIE. He's sick. He's got a sickness.

MOLLY. Should he be out there in a cold truck?

ARCHIE. He's not coming in here!

MOLLY. I'm not suggesting anything!

ARCHIE. I won't be able to eat.

(ARCHIE goes to MOLLY, kisses her, lightly. HE pats her bottom; lets his hand linger and rub.)

ARCHIE. I'll call you. (*Looks at her robe.*) Aren't you getting dressed, today?

MOLLY. As soon as they leave for school.

ARCHIE. I don't want to leave you not dressed.

MOLLY. So, wait.

ARCHIE. I can't wait. I've got to go.

MOLLY. As soon as they go to school, I'll get dressed. (*Cross left to stove.*)

ARCHIE. I don't like you traipsing around in front of everybody in a bathrobe.

MOLLY. What everybody? There's you, me, your mother, your father, our children! I'll get dressed as soon as they go to school.

ARCHIE. Fine. (*Reviews trucking papers at sideboard.*)

JACOB. T-t-t-take ...

RODDY. (THE YOUNGER) You're gonna hav'ta hop, Grandpa!

(*RODDY (The YOUNGER) tries, again, to extricate the cushion from under JACOB. ARCHIE sees.*)

ARCHIE. What are you doing to your grandfather?

RODDY. (THE YOUNGER) I'm trying to get his cushion out.

ARCHIE. Leave it! He needs his cushion for comfort!

RODDY. (THE YOUNGER) But, it's making him uncomfortable!

ARCHIE. Who says?

RODDY. (THE YOUNGER) He says!

ARCHIE. He said that?
RODDY. (THE YOUNGER) He did!
JACOB. *I* d-d-d ...
ARCHIE. So, take it out from under him.
RODDY. (THE YOUNGER) I'm trying to!

(JACOB hops up, RODDY falls to floor with cushion.)

ARCHIE. I'm leaving, now.
MOLLY. Kiss your father.

(ARCHIE offers his cheek to Roddy. (The Younger) to kiss. RODDY (The YOUNGER) kisses cheek.)

RODDY. (THE YOUNGER) Aren't you eating breakfast with us?
ARCHIE. Willie's sick.
JACOB. *(To Roddy.)* M-much B-b-b-better! Th-th-th ...
RODDY. (THE YOUNGER) You're welcome, Grandpa ... *(To Archie.)* Are you leaving right now?
ARCHIE. Right now. Why?
RODDY. (THE YOUNGER) I was kind of hoping I could try out my speech on you.
ARCHIE. Now?
RODDY. (THE YOUNGER) I was kind of hoping so.
ARCHIE. I can't, now. Willie's sick. *(Crosses upstage, puts on coat.)*

(HADDIE re-enters from upstage carrying newspaper.)

HADDIE. Here. Your paper. I froze getting it.

(Without pause, SHE goes to Jacob, lifts him by his collar, shoves cushion back under him; puts newspaper in his hands.)

JACOB. D-d-d-don't m-m-move m-m-me! ... *Dammit!*

HADDIE. What are you complaining about, you?

RODDY. (THE YOUNGER) I think he was more comfortable with the cushion out from under him.

HADDIE. What does *he* know? *(To Archie, as SHE sits.)* Why is your coat on?

ARCHIE. I have to leave early.

HADDIE. Why are you leaving early?

ARCHIE. Willie's sick.

HADDIE. I'm not surprised. *(Puts food on her and Jacob's plates.)*

RODDY. (THE YOUNGER) Do you think you could help me with my Red Feather speech, Grandpa?

JACOB. N-n-now?

RODDY. (THE YOUNGER) Well ... soon.

JACOB. A-a-ask your g-g-grandm-m-mother.

RODDY. (THE YOUNGER) Grandma, can Grandpa help me with my Red Feather speech?

HADDIE. Aren't you making yourself late for school?

RODDY. (THE YOUNGER) Why? What time is it?

HADDIE. Nearly seven-thirty. You shouldn't be speaking, now. You should be eating, now.

(RODDY sits at the table to eat.
Suddenly, MOLLY screams at Roddy (The Younger).)

MOLLY. Nearly seven-thirty, you, and still no socks on?

RODDY. (THE YOUNGER) I couldn't find any socks.

MOLLY. So, instead of looking and finding them, you're going to school with no socks?

RODDY. (THE YOUNGER) You were screaming at me to come downstairs!

MOLLY. No socks, like an *Italian*? (*Screams up staircase to Sylvie.*) Sylvie!

SYLVIE. What? What is it? What?

MOLLY. Come downstairs, you, and kiss your father goodbye!

SYLVIE. (*Off.*) Did you already eat without me?

MOLLY. Nobody ate anything! Your father's leaving early! Come downstairs and kiss him goodbye! (*To Roddy.*) There are clean socks in the airing cupboard! Put them on.

RODDY. (THE YOUNGER) What color?

MOLLY. Blue or brown, either color.

(RODDY exits, loping up staircase; MOLLY screams up to Sylvie.)

MOLLY. Your father is waiting to be kissed!

RODDY. (THE YOUNGER) (*Off.*) You just sent me up for socks!

MOLLY. I am talking to your sister!

ARCHIE. She doesn't have to, if she doesn't want to.

MOLLY. What are you saying, you? (*MOLLY moves to bottom of staircase; screams upstairs.*) What is taking you?

RODDY. (THE YOUNGER) (*Off.*) Me or her?

MOLLY. Her!

SYLVIE. (*From staircase.*) I was on the toilet!

(*MOLLY enters room; goes to Archie kisses Archie's cheek. MOLLY returns to stove.*)

SYLVIE. Why are you leaving before we eat breakfast?

ARCHIE. I've got to do something.

SYLVIE. In my whole life, you never missed eating breakfast with me, before, not once, not ever! ...

ARCHIE. I never eat with you on weekends ...

SYLVIE. School days, I mean school days ...

ARCHIE. I have to do something.

SYLVIE. What?

MOLLY. Don't pester your father!

(*SYLVIE sits at table.*

RODDY (The YOUNGER) enters carrying two pairs of socks: one red pair and one green pair.)

RODDY. (THE YOUNGER) There's no brown or blue, only red and green, and they smell bad.

MOLLY. Did you get those from the airing cupboard or the hamper?

RODDY. (THE YOUNGER) The hamper.

MOLLY. I said the airing cupboard!

RODDY. (THE YOUNGER) I wasn't listening.

ARCHIE. Give me a kiss. I'm going.

SYLVIE. I just kissed you!

ARCHIE. Him. I'm talking to him. (*To Roddy (The Younger)* Will you hurry, please?

RODDY. (THE YOUNGER) (*Goes to Archie; kisses Archie's cheek, again.*) Bye, Daddy. I hope you don't hit traffic.

ARCHIE. What smells bad?

RODDY. (THE YOUNGER) It's my socks. I got the wrong color.

MOLLY. Your son took dirty socks from the hamper.

RODDY. (THE YOUNGER) *Dirty*!? Oh, God! I *thought* they smelled funny! I'll put them back.

(RODDY (The YOUNGER) runs upstairs, as ARCHIE goes to Haddie; kisses her cheek.)

ARCHIE. Bye, Ma ... I'm goin'.

HADDIE. Goodbye, Arthur. I hope you don't hit traffic.

(ARCHIE goes to Jacob; touches his bald head, affectionately. JACOB looks at Archie disapprovingly. ARCHIE withdraws his hand; kisses his father's cheek.)

ARCHIE. Bye, Pop.

JACOB. B-b-bye ... I h-h-h-hope...

ARCHIE. The traffic will be fine, Pop ... (*To everyone.*) Well ...

(*Suddenly, there is a KNOCKING on the door. We can see the figure of a man, other side of curtains on door's window-pane. EVERYONE turns, stares; seems startled. No one moves or speaks.*)

WILLIE. (*Off.*) Arch?

(*ARCHIE breaks the in-house silence.*)

ARCHIE. I'm coming right out, Willie! ...

WILLIE. (*Off.*) I'm really feeling wick'id sick, Arch.

ARCHIE. Go back to the truck! I'll come right out!

WILLIE. It must be the Virus-X! I'm feeling really punk.

ARCHIE. Go back to the truck!

WILLIE. (*Off.*) Can you make it snappy, Arch? I'm really feeling *terrible*!

ARCHIE. I said I'm coming, didn't I? Go back to the truck!

WILLIE. (*Off.*) Okay, Arch, sorry ... I hate ta bother you when you're with your family and all ...

ARCHIE. (*Yells.*) When you're back in the truck, I'll come out! Not before!

(*There is a pause.*)

WILLIE. (*Off.*) Okay, Arch ... I'm goin'.

(After a moment's pause, ARCHIE speaks to his silent family.)

ARCHIE. I'd better start out.

RODDY. (THE YOUNGER) *(Re-entering, from stairs.)* Who was that at the door?

SYLVIE. *(Whispers.)* Willie.

RODDY. (THE YOUNGER) Oh.

ARCHIE. I'm starting out.

MOLLY. Kiss your father.

RODDY. (THE YOUNGER) I did, already!

MOLLY. Kiss him, again!

(RODDY kisses Archie's cheek; no hug.)

RODDY. (THE YOUNGER) Bye, Daddy.

(SYLVIE kisses Archie's cheek; no hug.)

SYLVIE. Bye, Daddy.

ARCHIE. *(To Molly.)* So?

(MOLLY kisses Archie full on the lips; big hug, moderate groping.)

ARCHIE. Are you going out, today?

MOLLY. Nothing special.

ARCHIE. You're sure on this?

MOLLY. I'm sure.

ARCHIE. Expecting any visitors?
MOLLY. Will you *please*?
ARCHIE. Yes or no.
MOLLY. Arthur ...
ARCHIE. Yes or no!?
MOLLY. Arthur!
ARCHIE. *Yes or no*?!
MOLLY. No!

(There is a pause.)

ARCHIE. It's Monday.
MOLLY. So, it's Monday.
ARCHIE. Your Mah Jong group isn't playing here?
MOLLY. My Mah Jong group isn't Mondays.
ARCHIE. So, when is it, then?
MOLLY. Tuesdays.
ARCHIE. Fine. I'm starting out. (*Looks at Molly; threateningly.*) I'll call you in an hour.

(WE HEAR: TRUCK'S HORN being tooted—three toots.)

ARCHIE. Bastard! (*Awkwardly.*) Well ... I'm off. (*ARCHIE goes to door, opens it, disappears outside. Five count. ARCHIE re-enters room.*) It's gonna rain. I need my slicker. (*HE grabs his raincoat from coat tree; goes to door; pauses.*) Well ... I'm off, again.

(ARCHIE exits. There is a small silence ... five count ... and then MOLLY takes full command.)

MOLLY. (*To Roddy (The Younger.*) You! Tie your shoes! (*To Sylvie.*) You! Pull up your knee-socks! (*To both.*) Both of you! Sit and eat your breakfast! You are not being late for school, again! Eat! (*Flashes looks at Haddie and Jacob.*)

HADDIE. We're eating!

JACOB. W-w-w-we're ee-ee-ee ...

MOLLY. Not you! Them!

(*ARCHIE re-appears at downstairs window, peering in from outside.*)

SYLVIE. Daddy, Mama.

(*MOLLY sneaks a peak at Archie ... sees him, looks away, quickly.*)

MOLLY. Oh, God! Smile, please!

(*MOLLY looks at her children and smiles her happiest smile. The CHILDREN join in, as do the GRANDPARENTS. The entire family is now smiling and eating breakfast, happily ... like a picture-book family. It's all for the benefit of Archie who spies on them.*)

MOLLY. (*To Haddie.*) Your son will put me in my grave!

HADDIE. (*Rises and gets milk from refrigerator.*) I hate to say it, but ...

MOLLY. Don't say it, then!

HADDIE. I have to say it!

MOLLY. So, say it.

HADDIE. My son is crazy. (*Pours milk and sits.*)

JACOB. (*Tries to yell at Archie, in window.*) G-g-g-get awa-awa-awa ...

MOLLY.	HADDIE.
Don't let him see you looking!	Don't let him see you looking!

JACOB. F-f-f-fine.

(*WE HEAR: TRUCK'S HORN being tooted, again—three toots. ARCHIE scowls, turns, exits from window.*)

RODDY. (THE YOUNGER) (*Rises and gets more juice from refrigerator. Crosses to window.*) He's gone.

MOLLY. Don't let him see you looking!

RODDY. (THE YOUNGER) He's gone!

MOLLY. Come, sit, you! Eat your breakfast!

(*RODDY (The YOUNGER) sits; joins family meal. MOLLY smiles at all.*)

MOLLY. Now, please, may we have ten consecutive seconds of sitting and eating in peace?

(*ARCHIE re-appears in downstairs den window, peering into his own house, discreetly spying on his family. He*

is framed in window as if on a giant TV screen.
SYLVIE is the first to notice Archie.)

SYLVIE. Daddy! ... *(Whispers.)* He's back, Mama.
MOLLY. *(Whispered.)* I see him.
RODDY. (THE YOUNGER) *(Whispered.)* He's back!
MOLLY. *(Whispered.)* I see him.
SYLVIE. *(Whispered.)* She sees him.
JACOB. *(Full voice.)* Ar-ar-ar ...
ALL except JACOB. She sees him!

(ALL begin eating, animatedly, enthusiastically, as though
Archie is not in the window.
After a moment, MOLLY covers her eyes, bows her head.
LIGHTS DIM in KITCHEN. RODDY (The
YOUNGER) stands, moves from table into spotlight,
downstage. RODDY (The YOUNGER) talks to
audience.)

RODDY. (THE YOUNGER) My father never left for
work, easily. He was always certain that what he called
"visitors" would be sneaking into our house, as soon as he
was gone. Because he drove his own truck, he was able to
drive by the house several times a day and pop in ... just to
check on things. We never knew exactly what kind of
"visitors" he expected to find in our house ... earthlings or
aliens. Only *he* knew for sure. And we never knew exactly
what purpose the visitors would have in our particular
house. What we did know, however, was not to be
frightened when a man almost always appeared, peeking in

through one of the ground floor windows, shortly after our father left for work ... or, shortly before our father got home from work. The fact is, it was kind of a shock the first time I had a sleep-over at Sal Cataldo's house, and his father, Mr. Cataldo, went straight to work and never once showed up in any of the downstairs windows. I also noticed that Sal and his father, Mr. Cataldo, both Italians, wore socks. And Mrs. Cataldo (who told me she was Irish before she got married) *used a napkin!*

(MUSIC IN: A romantic 1940's tune, sung by Sinatra or Crosby. LIGHTS FADE UP in KITCHEN behind RODDY (The YOUNGER). WE SEE: MOLLY and ARCHIE slow-dancing, cheek to cheek, sensually, romantically.
RODDY (The YOUNGER) looks into kitchen, watches his parents dance, for a moment. Then, HE smiles at audience.)

  RODDY. (THE YOUNGER) Things weren't always totally crazy between my mother and father. Sometimes, their romance was delicious. They loved to dance, cheek to cheek. Most of all, they loved to dance cheek to cheek *at home* ... in the *kitchen* ... after Grandma and Grandpa and Sylvie and I had gone to sleep. Sylvie and I would lie in our beds and hear Sinatra or Crosby, crooning ... and my mother and father, giggling.

(ARCHIE and MOLLY giggle ... kiss passionately, and exit up stairs. RODDY talks to audience.

RODDY. (THE YOUNGER) I'd better get to school. I'm going to practice my Red Feather speech in front of Mrs. Foxx, today. I'm competing in the Red Feather Oratory Contest at school. "We have nothing to fear but fear itself." ... That's the name of my speech. I didn't pick it. It was given to me by Mrs. Foxx. It's a quote from Franklin Delano Roosevelt. (*Simply.*) Franklin Delano Roosevelt was a crippled president who hated Jews.

(LIGHTS FADE TO BLACK.)

End of Scene 1

ACT I

Scene 2

MUSIC IN: A simple Chopin piano piece, simply played. LIGHTS FADE UP in KITCHEN, an hour later. MOLLY, still wearing robe, sits at piano, playing. HADDIE shuttles between table to sink, bringing dishes from table. JACOB sits in his chair, newspaper on lap, asleep.

HADDIE. If your husband catches you playing the piano, he'll be furious!

MOLLY. He won't catch me. (*SHE plays.*) It's a waste of good money to pay for lessons for one child, when, for the same money, the mother, if she's clever and she pays attention, can learn to play the piano, also. (*SHE plays.*)

HADDIE. If he comes back and catches you playing the piano, there will be hell to pay.

MOLLY. He won't catch me. (*SHE plays.*)

HADDIE. I won't protect you.

MOLLY. Fine. (*Stops playing.*) Are you happier?

HADDIE. I'm estatic.

MOLLY. Good. I'm glad. (*MOLLY goes to sink; dries dishes.*) Don't forget we're going out in a while.

HADDIE. When?

MOLLY. In a while.

HADDIE. Where?

MOLLY. Hmm?

HADDIE. Where are you going?

MOLLY. Where am *I* going?

HADDIE. That's what I asked: where are you going?

MOLLY. Out.

HADDIE. Alone?

MOLLY. Excuse me?

HADDIE. Are you going out alone? (*MOLLY turns, looks at Haddie, annoyed. HADDIE explains herself.*) If your husband comes home and you're out and I don't know exactly where or with who ...

MOLLY. (*Slips in correction.*) ... with whom ...

HADDIE. ... with *whom*, there will be trouble. And I, personally, couldn't give a fig where you're going or with whom, but, you can understand my demanding an answer, yes?

MOLLY. Did you wash this cup?

HADDIE. You certainly didn't.

MOLLY. It's filthy.

HADDIE. I think it's fine. If you think it's filthy, wash it again.

(MOLLY places cup in wastebasket.)

HADDIE. You threw the cup away?

MOLLY. It was filthy. If you don't want me to throw it away, take it out of the wastebasket and wash it.

HADDIE. It's a perfectly good cup.

MOLLY. The decision is yours to make.

(HADDIE goes to wastebasket, retrieves cup.)

HADDIE. It's not filthy.

MOLLY. Filthy.

HADDIE. It's a little soiled.

MOLLY. Drink from it, you'll be a little *diseased.* (*Sweeps floor.*)

HADDIE. Fine. (*Washes cup.*) You're not going to tell me?

MOLLY. I'm going swimming.

HADDIE. In this weather?

MOLLY. Yes, in this weather.

HADDIE. You want me to tell your husband you went swimming in this weather?

MOLLY. You wanna tell him I went swimming in *different* weather?

HADDIE. And with who?

MOLLY. With *whom*.

HADDIE. I hate that.

MOLLY. It's the object of a preposition.

HADDIE. I just hate that.

MOLLY. How do you expect the children in this house to speak English correctly, if the adults in this house don't speak English correctly?

HADDIE. They're your children. You want them to spend their lives worrying about propositions, this is your business. I'm just the grandmother.

MOLLY. Fine.

HADDIE. You didn't tell me with who.

MOLLY. With whom.

HADDIE. (*Annoyed.*) Fine. You didn't tell me with whom.

MOLLY. With you.

HADDIE. What are you giving me?

MOLLY. This is Monday. This is the day you and I are using the free trial passes they sent us for the new "Y" pool.

HADDIE. I forgot.

MOLLY. I only told you ten times.

HADDIE. I forgot. Next time, tell me twelve times! I'm an old lady. Shoot me.

MOLLY. You found your bathing suit?

HADDIE. I don't know.

MOLLY. You don't know if you found your bathing suit?

HADDIE. That is not it.

MOLLY. What is it?

HADDIE. (*After a thoughtful pause.*) I don't know.

MOLLY. What don't you know?

HADDIE. (*Discreetly; so that Jacob doesn't overhear.*) I don't know if I can parade around in a bathing suit at a YMCA, you know, in front of people.

MOLLY. (*Discreetly; a harsh whisper.*) Stay in the water. Don't parade. It's not a parading pool, it's a swimming pool.

HADDIE. Where am I supposed to put him while I'm swimming?

MOLLY. (*Sits at table with coffee.*) They have a creche with a full-time babysitter.

HADDIE. I'm supposed to leave him with children?

MOLLY. For a half hour! He can read his paper.

HADDIE. I don't know.

MOLLY. What don't you know, now?

HADDIE. (*Nods to Jacob. Sits at table with coffee.*) I've never undressed in front of him.

MOLLY. In front of who? ... Whom?

HADDIE. Your father-in-law. You see what I'm saying? If I've never undressed in front of your father-in-law, how can I undress in front of the world?

MOLLY. (*Shocked; faces Haddie, directly.*) Wait a minute, wait a minute, wait a minute! You've never undressed in front of your *husband*?

HADDIE. I change in the closet.

MOLLY. Wait a minute, wait a minute, wait a minute! You change in the closet?

HADDIE. None of this is anybody's business!

MOLLY. You change in the closet?

HADDIE. I think men and women should do things privately.

MOLLY. Does he change in the closet, too?

HADDIE. Not any more. The man can't even walk by himself. If I put him in the closet, I couldn't leave him in there, alone! ... He'd suffocate!

MOLLY. So, you change him, and then you go into the closet and change yourself?

HADDIE. Approximately.

MOLLY. My Goddd!

HADDIE. This is nobody's business.

MOLLY. Did your mother change in the closet?

HADDIE. With me?

MOLLY. That never occurred to me. Did she?

HADDIE. Of course not! Why would my mother change in the closet with me?

MOLLY. I don't know. Why would you change in the closet by yourself?

HADDIE. Because it's private!

MOLLY. Couldn't you change in the bathroom?

HADDIE. I'm done talking on this subject. (*Starts to rise.*)

MOLLY. (*Stopping her.*) Wait a minute, wait a minute, wait a minute, wait a minute! If your husband can't move on his own, why can't you just leave him somewhere where he can't see you, and then change? Why do you have to go into the closet?

HADDIE. This is really none of your business. (*Pauses.*) For one thing, I have to go in the closet, anyway, to get my nightgown. And in the morning ...

MOLLY. Your clothes are in the closet.

HADDIE. Exactly. (*Rises and rinses coffee cups.*)

MOLLY. (*Smiles.*) So, he's never seen you naked?

HADDIE. This is nobody's business.

MOLLY. Not even once?

HADDIE. Once or twice.

MOLLY. On purpose or by accident?

HADDIE. I won't dignify a question like that.

MOLLY. Fine.

(*HADDIE continues her dishes, wordlessly, for a few moments.*)

MOLLY. "Once or twice"? ... That's all?

HADDIE. I suppose you just change in the open?

MOLLY. He's your son. What do you think?

HADDIE. I couldn't begin to guess.

(*MOLLY considers what she's just learned about Haddie. SHE begins to laugh, aloud, quite joyously.*)

MOLLY. This is really *something!*

(*HADDIE looks at Molly, deeply annoyed. MOLLY, with some difficulty, stops laughing.*)

MOLLY. How many years have you and Pa been
living with us, now? Ten? Twelve?

HADDIE. Five.

MOLLY. That's all?

HADDIE. Five.

MOLLY. It seems like more.

HADDIE. Five.

MOLLY. It's seems like ten.

*(HADDIE notices that Jacob has been awake,
eavesdropping on their conversation. SHE screams at
Jacob.)*

HADDIE. Have you been listening to everything?
Have you been faking sleep and listening?

(JACOB laughs. HADDIE crosses up to Jacob.)

HADDIE. You are disgusting!

JACOB. (*Enraged.*) M-m-m-m-*meee*? I-I-I-*I'm* dis-g-g-
g...?

*(ARCHIE appears outside kitchen window, peering in,
spying on Molly, discreetly, mysteriously.)*

MOLLY. (*Sees Archie.*) Oh, God! He's back! Don't
turn around!

HADDIE. (*Sneaks a discreet peek.*) He must have
forgotten something.

MOLLY. Your son is driving me crazy!

HADDIE. For you, crazy is not a long drive.

(ARCHIE disappears from window.)

MOLLY. He's coming in!

HADDIE. *(To Jacob.)* Don't you tell him anything that we said, you!

JACOB. W-w-w-w-would I-I-I t-t-t...?

HADDIE. Shush, you!

(ARCHIE enters kitchen. HE playacts not seeing anybody downstairs; goes to staircase, yells upstairs.)

ARCHIE. I'm hooooommmme!

MOLLY. What are you yelling upstairs for? We're all right here.

ARCHIE. Oh. I didn't see you in here.

MOLLY. Something wrong?

ARCHIE. Uh uh. Why?

MOLLY. Truck troubles?

ARCHIE. Truck's fine.

HADDIE. Your wife's probably wondering why you're not working.

ARCHIE. Stay out of this, Ma!

HADDIE. Don't start in, Arthur!

ARCHIE. *(White-faced anger.)* Stay out of this!

JACOB. D-d-d-d-on't s-s-s-s.

ARCHIE. I want you in your bedroom!

JACOB. Ar-ar-ar-ar ...

ARCHIE. I want to talk to my wife ... alone!

(HADDIE shoots a look at Molly.)

MOLLY. It's okay, Ma.
HADDIE. Sometimes, I feel like I don't know my own son.
ARCHIE. Fine.
HADDIE. *(Goes to Jacob.)* Your son is banishing us from the room.
JACOB. I d-d-don't ...
HADDIE. Shah, you! Grab ahold.

(HADDIE lifts JACOB, "dances" him into bedroom. There is a moment's silence after they leave the room. MOLLY looks at Archie ... bravely.)

MOLLY. Let's have it.
ARCHIE. Is that a fresh mouth?
MOLLY. *(After a pause. Sits.)* No.
ARCHIE. I was riding with Willie up near the Stoneham line. He's sitting, dead quiet. I ask him, "What's up with the quiet?" ... He goes, "Ah, you know, Arch ... I'm feeling really sick with this virus-X and all." I say nothing on this. Then, no prompting from me, he goes, "Molly's looking wicked good, these days, Arch." I am stunned. *(Pauses, as if HE's dropped a bombshell.)* "Molly's looking wicked good, these days, Arch." Hmmmm? *(Pauses.)* I think this through for about a minute, and then I put the pieces together.

(ARCHIE walks around Molly, in a circle, wordlessly, staring at her ... looking her over.)

ARCHIE. Who are you meeting?

MOLLY. Excuse me?

ARCHIE. Who are you meeting means "Who are you meeting?" ... That's English I'm speaking, yes?

MOLLY. Meeting, where, Arthur?

ARCHIE. That's another thing I don't know. I don't know "Who" and I don't know "Where."

MOLLY. I'm not going anywhere and I'm not meeting anybody.

ARCHIE. Excuse me?

MOLLY. I'm not going anywhere and I'm not meeting anybody.

ARCHIE. *(Screams.)* I will not put up with this in my own house! I am working like a trojan, for what? So, I can go off with a derelict maniac in a truck and you can have meetings? Meetings? Do you think I'm stupid? *(No reply.)* Answer me! I asked you a question ... Answer me!

MOLLY. *(Quietly; holding back tears.)* What's your question, Arthur?

ARCHIE. Do you think I'm stupid?

MOLLY. *(Tears betray her courage.)* No, Arthur, I don't think you're stupid.

ARCHIE. *(Suddenly; to bedroom door.)* Get in here! *(No reply. Throws open bedroom door.)* I said "Get in here!"

(HADDIE enters from bedroom, head down, alone.)

HADDIE. What?

ARCHIE. Where was she planning to go?

HADDIE. What are you asking me, you?

ARCHIE. Nobody speaks English in this house? Where was she planning to go?

HADDIE. Where was who planning to go, Arthur?

ARCHIE. My wife: Where did my wife tell you she's planning to go?

HADDIE. She didn't tell me she was planning to go, anywhere, Arthur.

ARCHIE. Oh, but, she did ... Mother. *(Screams.)* TELL ME!

HADDIE. *(Frightened; the secret slips out.)* Swimming.

ARCHIE. Excuse me?

HADDIE. Swimming. Your wife is planning to go swimming.

(ARCHIE turns and faces Molly.)

ARCHIE. Swimming? You're going swimming? How interesting. *(Pauses.)* In the lake?

MOLLY. In the new pool, at the YMCA ... with your mother.

HADDIE. *(To Archie.)* I hadn't definitely agreed to go! *(To Molly.)* I didn't say "yes, definitely"!

MOLLY. Fine.

ARCHIE. I don't think so.

MOLLY. Fine.
ARCHIE. Fine, in what sense?
MOLLY. I won't go. I'll stay home.
ARCHIE. All day?
MOLLY. All day.
ARCHIE. You promise me this?
MOLLY. Yes.

(There is a substantial pause in which MOLLY looks down at her shoes, silently, seething, on the brink of tears. ARCHIE stares at her a moment; then, HE stares at HADDIE, who loses her courage; looks down. ARCHIE laughs. HE now goes to the piano, closes cover and WOMEN jump.)

ARCHIE. Was anybody playing the piano in here? *(No reply.)* I asked a simple question.
MOLLY. No.
ARCHIE. No, what?
MOLLY. Nobody was playing the piano in here.
ARCHIE. *(To Haddie.)* You agree?
HADDIE. *(After a small hesitation.)* No.
ARCHIE. No, what?
HADDIE. No, nobody was playing the piano in here.
ARCHIE. Really?

(WE HEAR: JACOB screaming from downstairs bedroom, off.)

JACOB. *(Off.)* She's l-l-lying!

(MOLLY and HADDIE wince; exchange a conspiratorial glance.)

ARCHIE. *(Smiles.)* How interesting.

(WE NOW HEAR: the sound of the TRUCK'S HORN, off. Three beeps.)

ARCHIE. Willie. The sex-fiend's got ants in his pants. *(Looks at watch.)* I have to go. We're already an hour late with this load. If the mill closes for lunch, before I get there, I'll be stuck in the truck with him for two extra hours. *(Goes to door; turns to Molly.)* We'll talk more about this piano-playing, later. *(Stares a moment, silently.)* I hope you're planning to put some clothes on, today.

(ARCHIE turns to the door, again, then, turns, again, looks at both women, then, turns to door a final time; exits. There is a pause. Then, ARCHIE appears at window, staring inside at his mother and his wife.)

MOLLY. Did God create men to curse women?

(The WOMEN exchange another glance; then, exit together, straight upstage, arm in arm.)

End of Scene 2

(THE LIGHTS CROSSFADE TO...)

ACT I

Scene 3

SPOTLIGHT on SYLVIE, sitting at piano. MUSIC IN:
   Chopin piece, played by SYLVIE, under.
RODDY (The YOUNGER) practices his speech, more or
   less for Sylvie's benefit.

RODDY. (THE YOUNGER) "We have nothing to
fear, but fear itself." That famous quotation from President
Franklin Delano Roosevelt may not make a lot of sense,
now, but, it made great sense to over a hundred million
Americans, just a decade ago, when this great Nation was
plunged into War with Hitler and many many other
maniacs ...

(SYLVIE turns, faces Roddy with a look that says she is
   somewhat disgusted by his attempt. RODDY turns
   from Sylvie, upset. HE sees his own reflection in the
   wall mirror; goes to it; starts over.)

RODDY. (THE YOUNGER) "We have nothing to
fear, but fear itself." Just a decade ago, when this great
Nation was plunged into War with Hitler and many many
other maniacs, Franklin Delano Roosevelt spoke that

famous quotation as he led America into a war to save the
Jews, even though President Roosevelt personally hated the
very Jews he was saving! (*HE pauses, himself disgusted by
this attempt. HE moves to mirror, nose to nose with his
own reflection; starts over.*) "We have nothing to fear, but
fear itself." That famous quotation was spoken by President
Franklin Delano Roosevelt as he and many many other
Jew-hating maniacs plunged this great Nation into War! ...
(*HE pauses, totally disgusted by this fresh attempt; rolls
eyes to Heaven.*) Shit!

(*SYLVIE stops playing piano, turns to Roddy, picking up
     conversation from sometime earlier, middle of a private
     thought.*)

     SYLVIE. And you're really, honestly not frightened of
him?
     RODDY. (THE YOUNGER) (*Turns upstage.*) Of
Daddy? Am I not frightened of Daddy?
     SYLVIE. No, of President Eisenhower!
     RODDY. (THE YOUNGER) Why should I be
frightened of President Eisenhower?
     SYLVIE. That was a joke, you *derr*!
     RODDY. (THE YOUNGER) Did you have the dream,
again?
     SYLVIE. Last night and the night before.

(*LIGHT SHIFTS to SPOT on RODDY. HE speaks
     directly to audience.*)

RODDY. (THE YOUNGER) Sylvie has this dream, all the time, in which my father wears a Nazi uniform around the house, and keeps asking if anybody's seen any Jewish girls hiding in the attic.

(LIGHTS restore.)

SYLVIE. Last night, I killed him.

RODDY. (THE YOUNGER) You killed Daddy?!

SYLVIE. *(Stops playing piano.) Shhhhh!*

RODDY. (THE YOUNGER) *(Whispers.)* You killed Daddy?

SYLVIE. Not really!

RODDY. (THE YOUNGER) I know that.

SYLVIE. I mean in my dream!

RODDY. (THE YOUNGER) I know that!

SYLVIE. I had a machine gun and troops.

RODDY. (THE YOUNGER) What kind of troops?

SYLVIE. Troops. Men ... soldiers ... working for me. He came upstairs looking for young Jewish girls, and he spotted me, ya know, reading, in my bed ... and he started goose-stepping and yelling really scary things in German ...

RODDY. (THE YOUNGER) And you killed him?

SYLVIE. I gave the order and the troops killed him.

RODDY. (THE YOUNGER) What about your machine gun?

SYLVIE. *(Looks up; weeping.)* After he was dead, I shot him, again.

RODDY. (THE YOUNGER) How many times?

SYLVIE. ... A lot.

RODDY. (THE YOUNGER) A *lot*? (*Whistles.*) Jesus, Sylvie. Jesus. (*Pauses.*) You really think you ever would?

SYLVIE. (*Weeping.*) Don't ask me that!

RODDY. (THE YOUNGER) Well, you know, I'm really curious, that's all. I mean, if he came at me in a Nazi uniform and all, goosestepping ... speaking scary things in German ... (*Pauses.*) Jesus, Sylvie, I'm glad it's you having the dream, instead'a me. (*Pauses.*) You wanna take a walk downtown with me?

SYLVIE. Uh uh. I wanna practice for a while, before they come home. (*SYLVIE turns to piano; plays.*)

End of Scene 3

(LIGHTS CROSSFADE TO...)

ACT I

Scene 4

SPOTLIGHT on RODDY (The ELDER), on stair-case. HE speaks to audience, directly.

RODDY. (THE ELDER) When I look back over my childhood, there are many, many high points to remember ... Humming "God Bless America," in my bathtub, under soapy water, for forty-seven seconds and not dying! ...

Getting Pesky and Williams to autograph mint-condition rookie cards in the same season! ... Homering against Lincoln School with two men on! ... The Red Feather Oratory Contest ... "We have nothing to fear, but fear itself." ... But, most of all, I remember the day when my father and I rode in his green '51 Chevy flat-bed truck, together, down to the Congo Church, where he pulled my sister Sylvie out of her Girl Scout meeting by her hair in front of the whole troop, plus, a bunch of visiting Boy Scouts.

(LIGHTS SHIFT TO RODDY (THE YOUNGER),
    downstage. HE takes over narration; speaks to audience,
    directly.)

RODDY. (THE YOUNGER) Sylvie was thirteen, and my father thought she had done something really bad with her friend, Robert Dutton, who Sylvie had promised my father she'd never talk to, again, a week after my father had caught Sylvie and Robert kissing on the sun-porch.

(LIGHTS SWITCH, suddenly, to RODDY (The ELDER),
    now playing ARCHIE.
ARCHIE faces SYLVIE, who sits on piano stool, center,
    sobbing. ARCHIE paces in circles, around the girl,
    railing at her. HADDIE stands behind JACOB, in his
    chair, upstage left. MOLLY stands at sink. ALL watch,
    silently, sadly.)

ARCHIE. (*Enraged.*) Marcus Rosenman's daughter went to Girl Scout camp for two months ... FOR TWO MONTHS! ... Do you know what happened to her? *Do you know what happened to her?* (*No reply.*) I asked you a question, young lady, and I am not hearing an answer!

SYLVIE. (*Sobs.*) What's your question, Daddy?

ARCHIE. Do you know what happened to Esther Rosenman?

SYLVIE. I don't know, Daddy.

ARCHIE. I'm sure you don't. Do you know what "prostitute" means?

HADDIE.	JACOB.	MOLLY.
Arthur!	D-d-d-d...	Stop, you!

SYLVIE. I don't know what that means.

ARCHIE. Oh, please, will you? Do you think I'm stupid?

(*SYLVIE sobs.*)

ARCHIE. I asked you a question!

SYLVIE. (*Sobbing.*) I don't know what "prostitute" means, Daddy! I don't! I really don't! I just know it's a really bad thing!

RODDY. (THE YOUNGER) (*To audience.*) At this point, my mother has usually had enough. She will step between my father and my sister and take control. After a moment, when it looks like my mother and father will finally kill each other, I will step in, get myself clobbered ... But, I will defuse the bomb.

ARCHIE. The thing I hate more than a young girl's looseness is a young girl's lying! ... And you are lying to me!

SYLVIE. I'm not!

(ARCHIE pulls SYLVIE, roughly, downstage; slams her down in kitchen chair; screaming.)

ARCHIE. You are lying to me!

SYLVIE. I'm not lying to you, Daddy! I'm not!

ARCHIE. Don't talk back to me, you!

(ARCHIE raises his hand, threatening to slap SYLVIE, who winces and sobs. Suddenly, MOLLY approaches Archie with an extremely impressive bread knife in her right hand.)

MOLLY. That's enough, you! You shut that mouth, now, you!

HADDIE.	JACOB.	SYLVIE.
Molly!	D-d-d...	Mama, nooo!

ARCHIE. What's this, you?

MOLLY. You stay back from her! You're a crazy person!

ARCHIE. *I'm* a crazy person?

MOLLY. You heard me!

ARCHIE. I'm not the one with a bread knife in my hand!

MOLLY. You've got a bread knife for a *tongue*, you! Humiliating your daughter in front of her friends! Hurting her! Calling her names like I've never heard in my life!

ARCHIE. You want a daughter like Marcus and Ruth Rosenman's daughter, fine, that's you, but, that's not me, sister! I would rather be dead, than live to see such a thing! Believe me, I know where your daughter learns to make secret meetings.

MOLLY. What "secret meetings"?

ARCHIE. Hah!

MOLLY. She was at a Girl Scout meeting ... with girls!

ARCHIE. Those were not boys, there, too? Those were girls dressed up like boys?

MOLLY. They were Boy Scouts!

SYLVIE. They were Boy Scouts, Daddy!

MOLLY. It was a co-ed meeting ... to make bird-houses!

SYLVIE. We were making bird-houses, Daddy.

ARCHIE. That wasn't Robert Dutton, there, next to you, who you promised me—PROMISED ME!—you would never talk to again as long as you live?!

SYLVIE. (*Sobbing.*) I didn't know he was going to be there, Daddy! I didn't know any of the Boy Scouts were going to be there!

ARCHIE. He was next to you! You and he were laughing!

SYLVIE. He told me a joke!

ARCHIE. I'll bet he did! (*His anger is building, quickly.*) *I'll bet he did!*

(ARCHIE is now violent; hand in the air, threatening Sylvie.)

    ARCHIE. *I'LL BET HE DID!*

    MOLLY. *(Moves in between Archie and Sylvie, bread knife firmly clenched in her hand.)* Back, you! Get back!

HADDIE.	JACOB.	SYLVIE.
Molly!	D-d-d-d ...	Mama, nooo!

    ARCHIE. Come on ... Come ONNNN! *(ARCHIE now raises his fist toward Molly, threateningly.)*

(RODDY (The YOUNGER) looks at audience, shrugs, then, suddenly, runs straight at his father.)

    RODDY. (THE YOUNGER) Get away from her! Get away from her! Get away from her!

(RODDY (The YOUNGER) shoves ARCHIE backwards, against the stage right wall.)

HADDIE.	JACOB.	MOLLY.
Roddy!	D-d-d-d ...	Roddy, noo!

    ARCHIE. Are you out of your mind, you?

(RODDY (The YOUNGER) shoves ARCHIE again.
ARCHIE slaps the boy, violently. RODDY (The YOUNGER) flies backwards, squeals; then, rushes at Archie again.)

RODDY. (THE YOUNGER) God damn you! God damn you! God damn you!

(ARCHIE laughs; then, suddenly, violently, backhands the boy, who flies backwards.)

SYLVIE. Daddy, don't!

HADDIE.	JACOB.	MOLLY.
Roddy!	Roddy! ...	Roddy!

(There is a moment of stunned silence.)

ARCHIE. *(Goes to Haddie.)* He hit me, first. I just had a physical reaction ... He hit me, and I hit him back. It was a *physical reaction*! *(To Molly. MOLLY moves away left putting knife down.)* I didn't want to hit him, but, he hit me, first, and I just hit him back. *(Goes to Roddy tries to help him up. RODDY pulls away; moves downstage.)* Get up. Roddy, get up. I'm sorry. I said it: I'm sorry. Now, come on, get up. Get up!

RODDY. (THE YOUNGER) *(To audience.)* At this point, my father will break down and sob, uncontrollably, begging everybody's forgiveness.

(Suddenly, ARCHIE starts to sob. His sobbing is enormous. His body heaves, racked with sorrow.)

ARCHIE. I'm sorry I get so mad. It's just that ... Oh, God, what is *wrong* with me?! I'm sorry. I apologize to everybody. I can't stop myself. I'm sorry. I am ...

RODDY. (THE YOUNGER) (*To audience.*) And Sylvie, instead of ordering her troops to fire ...

(*Suddenly, SYLVIE runs into Archie's arms, hugs him.*)

SYLVIE. Don't cry, Daddy! It's okay, Daddy! It's okay, Daddy! Don't cry, Daddy! Don't cry, Daddy! It's really okay.

ARCHIE. (*To Haddie.*) I'm sorry, Mama ... I get so mad all the time. I get so mad. I'm sorry, Mama ... I'm sorry, Mama ... I am.

HADDIE. (*Consoling Archie.*) It's fine, Arthur. No harm done. It's fine. It's fine, Arthur. It's fine. It's fine.

ARCHIE. (*To Jacob.*) What's the matter with me, Pa? Am I a crazy person who can't control his temper? I'm so sorry, Pa.

JACOB. (*Reaches out; pats Archie's hand.*) It's o-k-k-k-k ...

ARCHIE. Don't stop loving me, please, Molly, please. I'm so sorry. I'm so sorry. Don't stop loving me, please, Molly, please. I'm so sorry. I'm so sorry.

(*ARCHIE is really sobbing, now. MOLLY is somehow deeply moved. SHE opens her arms, moves to Archie.*)

MOLLY. Oh, God ... Come on. Come here.

ARCHIE. I get so mad all the time, Molly. I can't stop myself. I can't stop myself.

MOLLY. (*Cradles Archie's head in her arms. HE weeps.*) I know. I know. Shhhhh. Shhhhh. It's okay.

SYLVIE. (*Hugs Archie as well.*) It's okay, Daddy. Don't cry. Don't cry, Daddy. I love you so much, Daddy. Don't cry, Daddy. Please? Please?

(*The entire family, with the single exception of RODDY (The YOUNGER), gathers tightly around Archie consoling him, comforting him.*)

RODDY. (THE YOUNGER) (*To audience.*) The entire room is now filled with an unexpected tenderness from which I am totally and utterly ... *excluded.*

(*RODDY (The YOUNGER) moves slowly across kitchen floor to the staircase, past his family, unnoticed. As HE climbs the stairs, the LIGHTS FADE OUT.*)

End of ACT I

ACT II

Scene 1

*MUSIC IN. LIGHTS UP ON RODDY (The ELDER),
downstage, carrying chair and steering-wheel column
with gear-shift, which HE sets into position, downstage
center.*

RODDY. (THE ELDER) As my father never worked
weekends, I rarely had a chance to ride in the truck with
him ... except when school was closed for the odd,
indigenous Boston holiday like Patriots Day, or, say,
Cardinal Cushing's birthday. I also used to ride to the mills
with him on major Jewish holidays like Rosh Hashanah
and Yom Kippur. (*Pauses.*) Sylvie, never. In her entire life,
not once. (*Pauses.*) Sylvie and I weren't allowed to go to
school on Jewish holidays ... because we were Jewish. Of
course, we didn't ever actually go to synagogue, because
my father thought the local rabbi, who was a dentist, full-
time, and a rabbi, part-time, was only in the rabbinical
game to have secret meetings with many many married
Jewish women who were active in the Temple Sisterhood.
But, that's another story. (*RODDY (The ELDER) begins
to "drive" his truck ... acts shifting gears and turning
steering wheel.*) ... Because my father was himself raised as
a synagogue-going Jew, he felt that he had to somehow

observe the Holiday, even though he was in a truck, on a highway, far from makeshift temples and fornicating rabbis. So, he said his High Holiday prayers in his Chevy flat-bed, on the way to the Felulah Mill in Fitchburg, Massachusetts.

(RODDY (The YOUNGER) enters carrying another chair, sets it down beside Archie, sits; takes over the narration.)

RODDY. (THE YOUNGER) And I got to ride along with him ... and Willie.

(WILLIE enters, carrying a chair, which HE places, sideways, next to Roddy's chair. WILLIE sits with arm on chair-back, as if resting on truck window ledge. RODDY (The YOUNGER) is sandwiched between the two grownups in a truck-cabin designed for two. The truck lurches left ... and then, right. The three MEN sway, side to side, appropriately. Suddenly, WILLIE spots something. HE leans his head out of truck window, like a large dog. HE begins whistling and cat-calling to an IMAGINED FEMALE PASSERBY. NOTE: The actor who has been playing RODDY (The ELDER) is is now, again, playing ARCHIE.)

WILLIE. *(Five shrill whistles, first; then, screams.) Hey, hey, hey, heyyyy, Hedy Lamar! Where'd you get those gambinos! Wanna wrap 'em around my coconuts?! (Shrill whistles, again.)*

ARCHIE. Not in front of the boy, Willie!

WILLIE. (*Leans out of imagined window. Shrill whistles, again; screams to IMAGINED FEMALE PASSERBY, again.*) *Stuck-up, conceited bitch*! Stick your nose up in the air any higher and I'll hav'ta climb a tree to dick ya!

ARCHIE. Did ya hear me say "Not in front of the boy," Willie?

WILLIE. (*Leaning out, still glaring at IMAGINED PASSERBY.*) Oh, lookit that, Arch! I get it! She's *with* somebody, Arch! This is why we're not gettin' the time of day! ... There you go! This is the reason we're getting *nothin'* off'a her, Arch! Jesus, she's *kissin'* the lucky bast'id! (*Calls out to IMAGINED MAN.*) Hey, you lucky bast'id! Bring your mother and father around, and I'll *marry* them! OOoooo, Gawd bless us! She's tonguin' him, Arch! (*Calls out to IMAGINED COUPLE.*) Parlez-vous Frenchie kiss-kiss! Oui oui oui!

ARCHIE. Not in front of the boy, Willie, will ya?!

WILLIE. Roddy probably knows twice as much as us both, put together, Arch, huh?

(*WILLIE squeezes Roddy (The Younger)'s leg.*)

WILLIE. Don'tcha, Rod, huh? (*Tousles Roddy (The Younger)'s hair.*) I'll bet they don't call ya "Rod" for nothin', right?

ARCHIE. What are you? Demented?

WILLIE. Let the kid answer for himself. (*Tousles Roddy (The Younger)'s hair, again.*) I'll bet they don't call ya "Rod" for nothin', huh?

RODDY. (THE YOUNGER) I guess not.

ARCHIE. (*To Roddy (The Younger).* What are you saying, you?

WILLIE. (*Illustrates his point, graphically.*) I'm just sayin' I'll bet they don't call yo'r boy "Rod" for nothin'.

ARCHIE. I'm talkin' to him. Why do you think we named you Roddy?

RODDY. (THE YOUNGER) Because you had an Uncle Rodney who died, and you loved him, and you named me for him.

ARCHIE. (*To Roddy (The Younger).*) Exactly. (*To Willie.*) This is the way it's done in the Jewish faith, Willie.

WILLIE. Hey, listen, no problem, Arch.

(*Suddenly, WILLIE leans out of window; screams to new, IMAGINARY, FEMALE PASSSERBY.*)

WILLIE. *Is that your ass, or are you stealing basketballs?*

(*RODDY giggles.*)

ARCHIE. Not in front of the boy!

WILLIE. Hey, whoa, slow down, Arch, slow down, slow down, slow down! *Look, look, look, look, look!*

*(ARCHIE acts downshifting gears, slows and stops truck
... The three MEN playact watching IMAGINED
FEMALE PASSERBY walk across street in front of
truck. Their eyes follow her, slowly, from right to left.)*

ARCHIE. (*Laughs.*) You're right. She's stealing
basketballs.

(RODDY sees his father laugh; laughs loudly.)

WILLIE. Your boy's laughin', Arch! He gets it! Little
Rod gets the joke, Arch!

ARCHIE. What's so funny, you?

RODDY. (THE YOUNGER) I think she's stealing
watermelons.

WILLIE. (*Roars with laughter; tousles Roddy (The
Younger)'s hair.*) Watermelons, Archie! Did you hear your
kid? *Watermelons!*

ARCHIE. (*Unable to hide his pride.*) I heard him.

*(WILLIE looks out of window at OTHER IMAGINED
PASSERSBY; giggles, out of context; tousles Roddy
(The Younger)'s hair.)*

WILLIE. (*Philosophically.*) I'm gonna tell ya what's
really great about getting up at four o'clock in the mornin'
and riding a truck the way we do, Little Rod: What's really
great about getting up at four o'clock in the mornin' and
riding a truck the way we do is you get an opportunity to
see many, many first-shift female factory workers in many,

many neighborhoods. In Wakefield, Stoneham, Woburn, you get your many laundry-girls and dry-cleaning plant workers ... clean, starched uniforms. Oh, yummy yummy yum yum! You can just *taste* what's underneath!

ARCHIE. What is *with* you? Are you brain-damaged, or what?

WILLIE. Lynn, Beverly, Salem, Swampscott, Marblehead, Gloucester give you your many female fish-plant workers ... your female fish-stick packers and your female cutters. This is the other end of the globe from a point of view of clean hands kinda thing. Your female fish-plant workers are bloody and thinkin' about death all the time. They're also thinkin' "Life's tough, so, why not?" ... This makes them readily available to the passing stranger, especially, if he's a sharp dresser with a good sense of humor and a long stiff tongue such as *moi*!

(ARCHIE begins to rock forward and back, slowly, mumbling a Hebrew prayer, under his breath. WILLIE stops talking, looks at Archie.)

WILLIE. What's gives, Arch? You feelin' car-sick, again?

ARCHIE. I'm praying. It's a Jewish High Holiday!

WILLIE. No problem, Arch.

RODDY. (THE YOUNGER) *(Looks up at Archie.)* Me, too?

ARCHIE. Did you convert? Are you an Episcopalian, now?

*(RODDY (The YOUNGER) clasps his hands together,
closes his eyes ... imitates Archie by rocking back and
forth, slowly ... prays.*
*WILLIE stares at both of them for a few moments,
silently. HE, then, looks up at Heaven, "crosses"
himself ... and HE, too, begins to pray.*
*THEY all pray for a few moments, as ARCHIE continues
to "drive" the truck, millward.)*

ARCHIE. Red light.

*(ARCHIE acts pulling truck to a stop at imagined red
light.*
*THEY all continue to pray for a moment, until, suddenly,
WILLIE notices an IMAGINED BEAUTY in car
stopped next to them at red light. HE smiles to Heaven,
gratefully.)*

WILLIE. *(To God.)* My prayers have been answered!
(Leans out of window, speaks to IMAGINED BEAUTY.)
Hullo, Baby-Dollface! Whose little girl are you? [Wanna
suck a lollipop?]

*(ARCHIE and RODDY (The YOUNGER) are astonished.
BOTH stop praying. BOTH roll their eyes to Heaven.*
*LIGHTS SWITCH TO BLACK. After TWO COUNT,
LIGHTS RESTORE. WILLIE is gone, his chair is
empty.)*

RODDY. (THE YOUNGER) From time to time, Willie would go off on what my father would call "a sex fiend's errands," and my father and I would be left alone to talk about life, together. We were not what you might call *naturally comfortable* with each other.

ARCHIE. So, well, uh, Rod ... How's school?

RODDY. (THE YOUNGER) School's good, Dad.

ARCHIE. School's good, huh?

RODDY. (THE YOUNGER) Oh, yuh, school's good.

ARCHIE. That's good.

(There is a substantial pause.)

ARCHIE. How's your sister?

RODDY. (THE YOUNGER) Sylvie?

ARCHIE. Well, Sylvie's your sister, yes?

RODDY. (THE YOUNGER) Well, you see her as much as I do.

ARCHIE. Not as much. You see her after I go off to work and, you know, before I come home. And if I go to bed, early, you sometimes stay up talking to her and all.

(There is a small pause.)

RODDY. (THE YOUNGER) I think she's fine.

ARCHIE. You think so?

RODDY. (THE YOUNGER) I do. I mean she's never said she's *not* fine ... not to me, privately.

ARCHIE. I'm glad to hear this.

RODDY. (THE YOUNGER) (*To audience*.) After a minute or so of silence, while he tried to find a subtle way to ask me what he *really* wanted to ask me, he'd, well, *give up*, and just *ask* me ... straight out.

ARCHIE. Does your sister ever talk to you about her doing weird things with boys?

RODDY. (THE YOUNGER) Oh, God, never! I don't think she even *knows* any boys ... except, ya know, you, me and grandpa. Uncle Arnold.

ARCHIE. If she ever talks to you about doing weird things with boys, you'll say something to me, right?

RODDY. (THE YOUNGER) (*To Archie; quietly*.) Sure, I will.

ARCHIE. It's for her own good. You know this, yes?

RODDY. (THE YOUNGER) Sure.

ARCHIE. You promise me on this?

RODDY. (THE YOUNGER) Sure. I promise. (*Glances to Heaven, privately; grimaces*.)

ARCHIE. Your mother never says anything oddball to you, does she?

RODDY. (THE YOUNGER) Mama? Uh uh.

ARCHIE. Never?

RODDY. (THE YOUNGER) Mama? Never. (*Pauses*.) Grandma, neither. If either of them ever do, though, I'll tell you, right away.

ARCHIE. Good.

RODDY. (THE YOUNGER) (*To audience*.) We played endless variations on this particular theme of Sylvie, Mama and/or Grandma's saying and/or doing weird and/or oddballs things to and/or with men. And each time, when the interrogation was done, my father and I would ride through a thousand embarrassed pauses as pregnant as the harlot Sylvie of my father's wildest dreams. We shared these silences as though the passing landscape were somehow suddenly *intriguing*, as though we weren't suffering the pain of such shared *awkwardness*.

(ARCHIE and RODDY (The YOUNGER) now stare straight ahead, sadly, each avoiding visual or spiritual contact with the other. For this brief moment, each is undeniably alone, each is undeniably in pain.)

RODDY. (THE YOUNGER) It happened on an October morning. School was cancelled for a teachers' convention, and Willie was off God-knows-where doing God-knows-what to God-knows-whom. My father and I had done the morning mill-run to Fitchburg, without saying a single word. On the trip back home, on a back road, somewhere near Leominister, Massachusetts, my father broke the silence.

(ARCHIE looks at Roddy (The Younger). The BOY returns the look. THEY share a silent stare for a moment. Then, ARCHIE speaks.)

ARCHIE. Rod?
RODDY. (THE YOUNGER) Yes, sir?
ARCHIE. You like to play baseball, don't you?
RODDY. (THE YOUNGER) I do, yuh.
ARCHIE. Are you any good?

RODDY. (THE YOUNGER) I could be better. I guess.

ARCHIE. Can you hit?

RODDY. (THE YOUNGER) I can hit okay. I'm a great fielder ... Not ground balls, so much as fly balls. I can catch 'em.

ARCHIE. That's great. (*Pauses.*) It's a pain in the neck I don't get much of a chance to play ball with you.

RODDY. (THE YOUNGER) That's okay. Mama plays with me a lot. She can't really hit 'em hard, but, it's still practice.

ARCHIE. We don't do much, together, I mean.

RODDY. (THE YOUNGER) It's okay. (*Brightly.*) We get to ride in the truck, together.

ARCHIE. You like doin' this?

RODDY. (THE YOUNGER) Are you kidding me? I love this!

ARCHIE. (*Happily.*) Me, too.

(*BOTH stare straight ahead. BOTH are smiling.*)

ARCHIE. How's your Red Feather speech coming?

RODDY. (THE YOUNGER) Oh, well, it's okay.

ARCHIE. It's getting close, huh?

RODDY. (THE YOUNGER) Four weeks, three days ... (*Looks at Archie's wrist-watch.*) ... sixteen hours. (*Pauses.*) If I win my school, I get to go on to the subregionals, and maybe, you know, the New England Finals and all.

ARCHIE. (*Whistles, appreciatively.*) Big stuff, huh?

RODDY. (THE YOUNGER) Oh, yuh. The national winner gets a $2000 college scholarship. I could pay my own way kind of thing.

ARCHIE. Scared?

RODDY. (THE YOUNGER) Me? About the contest? Not too much. I just wish it was, you know, better.

ARCHIE. What was better?

RODDY. (THE YOUNGER) My speech.

ARCHIE. Wanna try it on me?

RODDY. (THE YOUNGER) You kidding?

ARCHIE. Naw. What the heck ... It's just us, riding, together ... two guys ... father and son kinda thing. We won't hit home-plate for at least an hour. How long is it?

RODDY. (THE YOUNGER) My speech? Three minutes.

ARCHIE. That's all?

RODDY. (THE YOUNGER) Oh, yuh. There's a time limit.

ARCHIE. That's all the whole speech is?

RODDY. (THE YOUNGER) Well, yuh ... yes. We also get an extemporaneous part to do.

ARCHIE. Oh, yuh, right.

RODDY. (THE YOUNGER) (*Senses Archie's confusion; explains, gently.*) That means they give you a subject, right then and there, and you have to make up a speech on that subject with no preparation ...

ARCHIE. Just sort of make it up on the spot kind of thing?

RODDY. (THE YOUNGER) Exactly.

ARCHIE. You're probably good at that.

RODDY. (THE YOUNGER) Oh, yuh. I'm better at that part than the prepared part ... you know ... "We have nothing to fear, but, fear itself" kind of thing.

ARCHIE. What's this?

RODDY. (THE YOUNGER) That's my prepared part. I could do some of it for you. I wouldn't have to do the whole three minutes. I could just do the start of it.

ARCHIE. No, no, no. Do the whole thing.

RODDY. (THE YOUNGER) Really?

ARCHIE. Sure. Why not? I mean, as long as we're doing things, together, we might as well do *whole* things, together, right?

RODDY. (THE YOUNGER) Well, yuh, *sure!* The thing is, I'm not really finished.

ARCHIE. Do whatever you've got.

RODDY. (THE YOUNGER) Well, okay ... (*Clears his throat.*) Are you sure you wanna hear this, Daddy? You don't have to! ... I mean, I've got plenty of other people who don't mind ...

ARCHIE. Come on! Let me hear it!

RODDY. (THE YOUNGER) Well ... okay ... sure. (*Clears his throat.*) "We have nothing to fear, but fear itself." That famous quotation was spoken by President Franklin Delano Roosevelt ...

ARCHIE. Roosevelt said this?

RODDY. (THE YOUNGER) He did, yuh.

ARCHIE. Roosevelt was a Jew-hating bastard!

RODDY. (THE YOUNGER) I know. I talk about this in my speech.

ARCHIE. You don't say "bastard" in front of your teacher, do you?

RODDY. (THE YOUNGER) No, no. I use a different word.

ARCHIE. Let me hear.

RODDY. (THE YOUNGER) "We have nothing to fear, but fear itself." That famous quotation was spoken by President Franklin Delano Roosevelt as he and many many other Jew-hating maniacs plunged this great Nation into War! ...

ARCHIE. "Maniacs" ... good ... I like "maniacs."

RODDY. (THE YOUNGER) I tried it different ways, but, I liked "maniacs" best of all. Maybe I should wait till I get it finished more.

ARCHIE. No, no, no. I like hearing your speech. I like doing this ... just us kinda thing.

RODDY. (THE YOUNGER) (*Does the first part, again, rapidly, skipping over the lines to get to the yet-unspoken lines.*) "We have nothing to fear, but fear itself." That famous quotation was spoken by President Franklin Delano Roosevelt as he and many many other Jew-hating maniacs plunged this great Nation into War! ... (*Having re-capitulated the start of the speech, RODDY now slows his delivery down to a proper pace.*) What did President Roosevelt mean, exactly, when he uttered that famous quote? Did he mean that the things that scare us most aren't real? That they're imagined things ... like ghosts and boogey-men, which we, after all know aren't real?...

ARCHIE. Ghosts may be real.

RODDY. (THE YOUNGER) You think so?

ARCHIE. I dunno. I have this really weird kinda sense of my Uncle Herman all the time ... He was a Rabinowitz, on my mother's side. Uncle Herman Rabinowitz was kind of, you know, crazy. He was actually very crazy. He used to whistle in public ... patriotic marches ... from Poland. I think they were from Poland. He was arrested for exposing himself. You know what that means?

RODDY. (THE YOUNGER) Not exactly ... kind of. Like showing your private parts to people kind of thing?

ARCHIE. Sort of ... it means, more like showing your private parts to people who don't really want to *see* your private parts kind of thing.

RODDY. (THE YOUNGER) Oh, sure, right ... I get you.

ARCHIE. Uncle Herman Rabinowitz did this a lot.

RODDY. (THE YOUNGER) Gosh.

ARCHIE. He was arrested. Uncle Herman said he was peeing, but, the lady who turned him in said he was doing more than that. (*Pauses.*) Don't ever tell your grandmother I told you any of this stuff, okay?

RODDY. (THE YOUNGER) I won't! ...

ARCHIE. You've gotta promise!

RODDY. (THE YOUNGER) I promise!

ARCHIE. Good.

RODDY. (THE YOUNGER) Would you mind if I waited to show you the rest of my speech 'til I've done a little more work on it?

ARCHIE. Hey, you're the boss! It's *your* speech.

RODDY. (THE YOUNGER) Really?

ARCHIE. Sure!

(There is a moment's pause, during which BOTH MEN are smiling. Then, RODDY pops The Big Question.)

RODDY. (THE YOUNGER) When do you think you could teach me to steer?

ARCHIE. You're not s'posed'ta touch a wheel 'til you're sixteen! ... You're not allowed! This is Massachusetts! I could go to jail for letting you steer! Sixteen's the law! ...

RODDY. (THE YOUNGER) You told me Grandpa taught you to steer when you were my age.

ARCHIE. That was different. We had no money. *(ARCHIE acts pulling truck over to side of road; stops truck.)* Come on over here.

(RODDY (The YOUNGER) squeezes into ARCHIE's "embrace," as RODDY clutches steering wheel and ARCHIE guides him ... RODDY pretends to steer truck. BOTH MEN are, for the moment, very, very happy.)

RODDY. *(To audience.)* We rode together that way, me steering ... he, with his arms around me, guiding me, sharing an against-the-law risk with me for at least four minutes.

ARCHIE. That's enough now.

(ARCHIE stops the truck; RODDY (The YOUNGER) relinquishes the steering wheel, slides away from Archie; looks out to audience, directly.)

RODDY. (THE YOUNGER) In my entire childhood, I only remember my father hugging me that one time.

End of Scene 1

(THE LIGHTS CROSSFADE TO...)

ACT II

Scene 2

HADDIE shuffles on, calls out to Roddy (The Younger).

HADDIE. Okay, Roddy, I'm ready to listen to your speech, now.

(HADDIE moves to stove, makes cup of tea for herself, as RODDY (The YOUNGER), moves to her, practicing his speech.)

RODDY. (THE YOUNGER) Okay, Grandma ... Here goes ... What President Roosevelt was teaching us was to get over our fears, before they cripple us ... the way polio crippled *him*—Roosevelt—who was a cripple. So, when Roosevelt says "We have nothing to fear, but fear itself," he's telling us to find the courage to confront the thing itself instead of our fear of the thing itself, before we, ourselves, become crippled like Roosevelt, who, of course, got crippled by polio, not fear. (*Pauses, confused; disgusted by still another lamentable failure. HE mouthes an appropriate word, behind his Grandmother's back silently.*) [Shit!]

    HADDIE. Maybe you shouldn't type it up, just yet.

(*HADDIE takes tea bag from teacup, tosses tea bag into wastebasket, crosses upstage to kitchen table; sits, waits for Roddy to join her.*
The LIGHTS CROSSFADE with RODDY (The YOUNGER), who moves quickly into SPOTLIGHT, downstage right; speaks to audience, directly.)

    RODDY. (THE YOUNGER) Just before my Grandma Haddie died, she told me the most amazing thing about my family, Grandpa Jacob included.

(*LIGHTS CROSSFADE from RODDY back to HADDIE. RODDY crosses to table, sits in chair beside Haddie.*)

    HADDIE. The men in our family are crazy people, all of them! They think every woman is loose! My own father, may his soul rest in peace, used to make my mother wear an overcoat, all through the summer, so, no man could see that she had big breasts. In the meantime, my father's own uncle, Duddy, on the Zuckerman side, may his soul never rest a minute, used to touch me in private places, when I was a very little girl. His wife said he used to light fires in front of pictures of naked ladies. Your own grandfather is no picnic, himself. In all the years we've been married, which is forty-seven, he has never once let me shop, alone. He was not only convinced the butcher was after me, he was also convinced that I was after the butcher! Once, he kicked a hole in the dining room wall, because I let the butcher sell me an extra-lean rib-roast. (*Shrugs.*) Go figure! ... (*Continues.*) I used to tell him "You're just like your father!" and this would always drive your grandfather crazy, because he really hated his father, your great-grandfather, who used to yell things at women on the street that you should never know about! God forbid! ... I'm going to tell you something, Roddy. No matter how crazy your grandfather got when I told him he was like just his father, I'm telling you he was *just* like his father! Maybe worse. Your own father (my son), I don't have to tell you much about, because you're *living* in the story, yourself, yes? But, I have to tell you one story ... from the zoo in Stoneham, when he was little. Your grandfather and I took him there on a very sunny Sunday morning. There was a crowd in front of the lion's cage and we were way at the back ... So, Arthur, your father, squeezed in through the people, up to the front, all by himself. When he got there—to the front—for some reason, the lion roared. It was really quite a roar. Long, loud, really enormous. Everybody—all of us, kids and grownups, got scared. And then we all laughed. But, I

knew your father would have gotten very scared, so, I
pushed my way up front. When I got to him, he was off to
one side, roaring like a lion. There were tears all over his
face and his sailor-shirt, but, he was roaring, really loud,
just like the lion. The sound coming out of him was
enormous. I let him roar for a while, until he got himself
calmed down. (*Pauses.*) Sometimes people do this, Roddy
... Sometimes, people have to imitate the things that scare
them the most. (*HADDIE pauses; moves to Roddy; speaks
to him, confidentially.*) I'm only telling you any of this,
because, between us, I don't like these shooting pains in
my head I'm getting, and somebody's got to talk straight
to you, before you, yourself, start, you know, roaring.

RODDY. (THE YOUNGER) I'm never going to do
any roaring, Grandma.

HADDIE. Fine. I'm glad to hear this, but, maybe you
should try to remember my story, just in case you ever
hear yourself roar a *little*.

RODDY. (THE YOUNGER) I will.

HADDIE. Good.

RODDY. (THE YOUNGER) You have pains in your
head, Grandma?

HADDIE. This is between us. Promise me.

RODDY. (THE YOUNGER) I promise you. (*Pauses.*)
I'm sure you're going to be fine, Grandma!

HADDIE. Maybe I don't *want* to be fine? Maybe
enough is enough. (*Pauses; smiles.*) Let me say what I'm
trying to say to you, simply and clearly, Rodney ... All of
the men in this family are crazy people. Wait. You'll see.
(*HADDIE's LIGHT FADES OUT. End of Scene 2.*)

ACT II

Scene 3

RODDY (The YOUNGER) moves into spotlight, downstage, right; speaks to audience, directly.

RODDY. (THE YOUNGER) We always thought Grandpa would die before Grandma. I guess we *hoped* he would. So, when Grandma died, like she did, before Grandpa, we didn't know what we were going to do with him.

(LIGHTS CROSS-FADE with RODDY (The YOUNGER) as HE moves to Jacob. Offstage, WE HEAR: the sound of "Kaddish," the Hebrew prayer for the dead.)

RODDY. (THE YOUNGER) We should go back into the front room, now, Grandpa. They're saying "Kaddish," again.

JACOB. They've got their ten men. They've got *twenty* men! (*Leans in, discreetly.*) Your grandmother had a lot of men-friends, Roddy.

RODDY. (THE YOUNGER) You think so?

JACOB. I *know* so. (*Looks at Roddy, smugly.*) That's all I'm going to say on this subject.

RODDY. (THE YOUNGER) (*To audience*.) Grandpa
Jacob's Parkinsonian stutter cleared up the minute Grandma
Haddie was in her grave.

JACOB. It was hell being married forty-seven years to
a beauty like your grandmother, Roddy. If I can give you
one piece of advice, straight from my heart, when you're
ready to get married, find the ugliest woman you can find
... somebody so horrible other men will avert their eyes
when she passes. This woman, if she has any brains at all,
will know how unappealing she is to the male multitude,
and she will love you for marrying her ... And she will
serve you, without any of the pain I had with a beauty like
your grandmother. This is advice from my heart, Roddy. I
gave this advice to your father and he didn't take it, and
now look at him!

*(JACOB motions to window. ARCHIE is outside, peering
into the house, suspiciously. RODDY (The Younger)
moves toward window. ARCHIE quickly disappears
from the window.)*

RODDY. (THE YOUNGER) Do you think all of the
men in our family are crazy, Grandpa?

JACOB. Did your grandmother suggest this to you?

RODDY. (THE YOUNGER) She did, yes.

JACOB. Your grandmother knew a lot about people,
Rodney ... especially, men!

*(WE HEAR: the sound of MALE VOICES singing
"Kaddish" ... the Hebrew prayer for the dead. MOLLY*

enters. SHE is in mourning, wears a black dress; calls out to Jacob.)

MOLLY. Let's get you in here, Pa! They're saying "Kaddish"!

JACOB. (*Screams, suddenly.*) For *her*, not for *me*! I'm not dead!

MOLLY. Who said you were dead? (*To Roddy (The Younger.*) Did I say such a thing?

RODDY. (THE YOUNGER) It's the prayer for Grandma, Grandpa. Come on, I'll go inside with you.

JACOB. No! You're just a young boy! I don't want you in there! Young boys shouldn't have to see such things. (*Motions to Molly.*) She'll take me in.

MOLLY. Come on, Pa. Grab ahold.

(MOLLY leans in, places JACOB's hands on her shoulders, starts to lift him from his chair. JACOB begins to cry; yells at Molly, directly.)

JACOB. How could she leave me alone by myself with people like *you*? How *could* she? *How*?

(WE HEAR, again, MALE VOICES singing "Kaddish," under the scene, as JACOB continues to sob, openly, now, calling Haddie's name, in German/Yiddish.)

JACOB. Haddelah ... mein Haddelah ... Haddelah ... liebling ...

MOLLY. (*Quietly.*) Come on, Pa ... I'll take you in.

(MOLLY leads JACOB into room. HE walks forward, SHE walks backward ... as if in a waltz.)

RODDY. (THE YOUNGER) *(To audience.)* Grandpa Jacob died that night. We all heard it ... his scream. It would have been too corny, even for Grandpa Jacob's favorite radio show, "Portia Faces Life."

JACOB. *(Screams, from off, from the darkness.) I don't want to live without her! Arrrrhhhh!*

RODDY. (THE YOUNGER) We knew he would be dead when we went in there.

(LIGHTS UP in KITCHEN, suddenly, on switch, SYLVIE and MOLLY run down stairs to door of back bedroom; stop before entering.)

MOLLY. *Pa?*
RODDY. (THE YOUNGER) *Grandpa!*
SYLVIE. *Grandpa!*
ARCHIE. *(Off.) Paaa?*

(ARCHIE runs down stairs, crosses kitchen to Jacob's bedroom, runs inside. Beat. HE screams.)

ARCHIE. *(Off.) Paaaaaaaaaaaa!*

(MUSIC IN: WE HEAR, again, MALE VOICES singing "Kaddish," offstage.

*RODDY (The YOUNGER), SYLVIE, ARCHIE and
MOLLY stand framed in doorway to Jacob's bedroom.
THEY bow their heads and weep, as MUSIC
CONCLUDES.)*

End of Scene 3

(LIGHTS CROSSFADE TO...)

ACT II

Scene 4

*SPOTLIGHT, downstage center on RODDY (The
YOUNGER), who faces audience. MUSIC IN: Chopin
etude, played on piano, lightly.*

RODDY. (THE YOUNGER) The night after Grandpa
Jacob died, I was laying awake, thinking about things, and
it crossed my mind that when Roosevelt said "We have
nothing to fear, but fear itself," he could have been
completely full of shit! We have *plenty* to fear! ... We have
old age to fear. We have loneliness and disease to fear. We
have some very crazy people around us all the time to fear!
We also have things like Red Feather Oratory Contests to
fear! And we also have The Worst to fear. (*Pauses.*) The

Worst happened to me and my family on the morning of
the Red Feather Regionals. If I live to be sixty, I will
always wonder if either Grandpa Jacob or Grandma Haddie
had lived just a little longer and had been alive that day ...
if either of them had been, you know, home in the house
with Mama, whether it would've changed anything ... Or
whether all bad things are *meant to happen* and they just
do: they just *happen*, no matter what.

*(LIGHTS WIDEN, lighting KITCHEN and MOLLY at
    piano, playing Chopin. SHE is wearing her bathrobe
    and bedroom slippers.*
*A MAN is peering through the upstage right window into
    the house from outside. NOTE: audience should assume
    the MAN is ARCHIE. The MAN disappears from
    window, as suddenly as HE had appeared.*
*RODDY (The YOUNGER) continues speaking to the
    audience, directly.)*

RODDY. (THE YOUNGER) He must have come into
the house around around ten-thirty in the morning. Sylvie
and I were both in school. What I remember most of all
about the day was that I learned about Congressional
franking privileges. Sylvie says she has no memory of the
day, whatsoever. Daddy was supposed to be with Willie in
Fitchburg, unloading the truck. But, Willie had called in
sick with the Virus-X.

*(The MAN, suddenly, reappears at other window, peers in
    at Molly. We now see that it is WILLIE in window,*

*not Archie. MOLLY continues to play, oblivious to
WILLIE in window.*
*WILLIE disappears from window, suddenly; then, reappears
at door. HE KNOCKS on door, three times. MOLLY,
intent on her piano playing, doesn't hear him.)*

RODDY. (THE YOUNGER) There are moments that
re-define an afternoon, and there are moments that re-define
a life. This was, alas, a moment to re-define the my entire
family.

*(RODDY (The YOUNGER) exits up staircase, as WILLIE
enters house, stops and watches Molly play.*
*MOLLY senses Willie's presence in room and, certain it is
Archie who has entered, SHE whirls around, away from
piano.)*

MOLLY. I was only seeing if the piano was out of
tune! ... (*Sees it's Willie, not Archie.*) Willie.

WILLIE. I didn't know you played piano. You play
wicked good, don't'cha?

MOLLY. (*Re-belting her robe, tightly.*) You shouldn't
be in the house, Willie.

WILLIE. I was feelin' a lot better after my nap, so, I
hopped on over here to see if I could catch Arch before his
second mill-run.

MOLLY. Archie's not here. He left over an hour ago.

WILLIE. (*Appreciating her body.*) Archie never talks
about you playing the piano, Moll. Never mentions it,
ever. You play Classical, too. Sophisticated. (*Looks*

around room; smiles.) It's nice bein' in the house with you, just us, like this. It's a shame about Archie's folks and all. Still and all, they lived life, didn't they. I mean, that's what life's for, ain't it ... livin'. Ain't it, Moll? (*Sits in Jacob's chair. Looks Molly over.*) You're lookin' good, Molly. I was just sayin' this very thing ta Arch, not all that long ago: Molly's lookin' wick'id good. (*Laughs; looks Molly over, again.*) You really are lookin' wick'id good, Moll. You're puttin' on weight in all the right places. Not that you're lookin' heavy. I ain't sayin' that. You're lookin', I dunno, what's the word? ... Comfortable. Some women are built for speed, but, you're very definitely built for comfort.

MOLLY. You shouldn't be in the house, Willie. You're not allowed. You know this.

WILLIE. *Allowed*? I'm not *allowed*? (*HE laughs. Rises.*) That's a funny thing you just said, Moll. (*Moves to door of back bedroom; peeks inside.*) This is where they slept, huh? The old ones. (*Smiles at Molly.*) Must be lonely in the house for you, now, huh, Moll? ... Kids at school ... Arch off somewhere in the truck as he is ... Just a good-lookin' girl like you, alone, in a big house like this. (*Moves to staircase; looks upstairs.*) I never be'n upstairs. Weird, huh? All these years workin' for Arch and all, and I never be'n upstairs in his house. I mean, he's be'n upstairs in *my* house, plenty, right?

MOLLY. You can't be in the house, Willie. You're going to have to leave, now.

WILLIE. I don't think so.

MOLLY. Willie, please! I must insist you leave the house.

WILLIE. (*Stares at Molly; smiles.*) Uh uh.

MOLLY. Willie, please? I'm asking you, nicely. (*SHE opens door for Willie to leave.*)

WILLIE. Oh, well, if you put it that way ... (*WILLIE starts to door, as if HE's leaving ... but, then HE slams door closing, confronts Molly.*) Not a chance. (*Sees MOLLY looking about, furtively.*) How come you're talking like somebody else is listening? Nobody's listening! It's just us.

(*WILLIE caresses Molly's cheek, pushing her hair out of her eyes. MOLLY is stunned. She cannot possibly misinterpret Willie's intentions. SHE steps backwards from him, stiffly.*)

MOLLY. Willie, get out of this house!

WILLIE. (*Moving toward her, again.*) You like me, don't you, Moll?

MOLLY. If you don't leave, *I'll* leave.

(*MOLLY starts to door. WILLIE blocks her path.*)

MOLLY. Willie, get out of my way! ... I want to go outside.

WILLIE. In your bathrobe? You wanna go outside in your bathrobe, Molly?

(WILLIE starts to move slowly toward Molly, laughing. MOLLY backs up, terrified.)

MOLLY. Willie!

WILLIE. I seen you lookin' at me, for years and years, now, four mornin's a week, never changin' outta your bathrobe 'til after I'm gone and all, right? ... Flashing this and that at me ... Smilin' at me, makin' my lunches and all ... Askin' all the time if my coughs and colds are gettin' better kind'a thing! I seen and felt all this *attraction* coming from you, Moll.

(WILLIE steps forward, tries to embrace Molly. SHE slaps his face. It is a stunning blow. WILLIE staggers backward, shakes his head clear; laughs.)

WILLIE. I knew you'd fight me!

(WILLIE steps in, grabs Molly, firmly, tries to kiss her. SHE wriggles and screams, trying to get loose from him. Suddenly, the door opens; ARCHIE enters the kitchen. HE is ashen.)

WILLIE. Jesus, Arch! You look wick'id pissed! ... Take it easy, Arch, huh? I can explain myself, here! ... She invited me in, Arch. I would'a gladly waited outside, like you said, but, she ...

(ARCHIE moves past Willie, wordlessly; goes directly to Molly; slaps Molly. SHE screams; falls backwards

*against table. ARCHIE slaps her, again. WILLIE stares
at Archie, amazed.)*

WILLIE. Jesus, Arch! What are you doin'? What are
you hittin' her for?

*(ARCHIE never looks at Willie. Instead, HE slaps Molly,
again.)*

ARCHIE. Your boyfriend's askin' what I'm doing.
You hear him?

(MOLLY doesn't reply.)

ARCHIE. You're not answering me?

(No reply. ARCHIE slaps Molly, again.)

WILLIE. *(Horrified.)* Jesus! Nothin' happened between
us, Arch! Honest ta God! You gotta calm yourself down,
Arch, before you do damage!
ARCHIE. Whoaaa! You hear this?

(No reply. ARCHIE slaps Molly, again.)

ARCHIE. Your boyfriend's protecting you. Do you
not hear him?

(ARCHIE raises his hand to hit Molly, again. WILLIE reaches in to stop him; barely touches ARCHIE, who recoils from his touch, violently.)

ARCHIE. No touches, you! *No touches!* (*ARCHIE slaps Molly, again.*) Every time your boyfriend protects you, you're getting hit! You get me! *You get me?*
WILLIE. Jesus, Arch! ... Jesus! (*WILLIE turns, runs out of door; exits play.*)
ARCHIE. (*In a murderous rage; stands ready to hit Molly, again.*) I seen this coming, lady, believe-you-me! You couldn't even wait 'til my mother and father were cold in the grave, could you? Could you? *Could you?* (*ARCHIE raises his hand; moves to hit Molly.*)

(THE LIGHTS BLACK OUT, on SWITCH.)

End of Scene 4

ACT II

Scene 5

In the darkness, WE HEAR: MICROPHONE "FEEDBACK" and then ... ANNOUNCER'S VOICE over public address system, heavy Boston accent.

ANNOUNCER'S VOICE. Ladies and Gentlemen, our next competitor in The Red Feather Oratory Contest New England Finals is our youngest competitor. He is a fifteen-year-old high school student from Wakefield, Massachusetts. Welcome, please, Rodney Stern!

(WE HEAR: Applause. SPOTLIGHT FADES UP on RODDY (The YOUNGER), upstage, near piano. HE delivers his Red Feather Oratory Contest speech ... with poise, confidence ... and appropriate hand-gestures.)

RODDY. (THE YOUNGER) Fellow Red Feather Oratory Contest competitors, Judges, Ladies and Gentlemen ... "We have nothing to fear but fear itself." When President Franklin Delano Roosevelt spoke those words, he was trying to trick the citizens of the United States of America into finally going to War against Hitler. FDR knew America should have gotten into the War, years and years before, but, Roosevelt was waiting as long as he could, hoping that Hitler would kill all the Jews, first, because Franklin Delano Roosevelt, like Adolph Hitler, hated the Jews. Finally, after the Japanese bombed Pearl Harbor and killed some non-Jewish Americans, Roosevelt knew he couldn't wait any longer. He declared War on Japan ... and on Japan's teammate: Hitler. *(Pauses.)* The only thing that's kept a lot of people from saying all this stuff about Roosevelt out loud is fear. I myself felt a lot of fear thinking about saying this out loud in my Red Feather Oratory Contest speech, but, it's the truth, and nobody should ever be frightened to speak the truth, should they?

(RODDY (The YOUNGER) pauses, allowing his question to hang on the air.)

(THE LIGHTS FADE UP in the KITCHEN. MOLLY enters, carrying two suitcases, which SHE sets down on floor near back door. SHE is badly bruised; battered. SHE busies herself, preparing to close up the house. SHE checks to see that the gas is off, water faucets are tightly shut, windows are closed and locked, etc.)

RODDY. (The YOUNGER) ... To be heroic, you first have to be unlucky enough to find yourself in a terrible situation ... and then, you have to be lucky enough to find your dignity ... and that will lead you to do what you have to do.

(WE HEAR: A CAR HORN, offstage.)

RODDY. (THE YOUNGER) *(Calls out to his mother.)* The taxi's here!

(MOLLY opens back door; calls outside to imagined taxi driver.)

MOLLY. We'll be right out! ... *(SHE moves to base of staircase; calls upstairs.)* The taxi's here! Are you ready?

(SYLVIE calls down from upstairs.)

SYLVIE. *(Off.)* I'm ready! ...

RODDY. (THE YOUNGER) (*To audience*.) Sylvie went downstairs, first. I hung back in my room and hid a copy of my Red Feather Oratory Contest Speech under a loose floorboard in my closet. I started down the stairs, but, then, I ran back to my room and tossed my signed Williams and Pesky rookie cards under the floorboard with my speech! ... I don't know why I did that. It's one of my life's few major regrets.

(SYLVIE enters from upstairs. SHE, too, wears a winter overcoat. SHE, too, carries suitcase. SHE, too, has been crying.)

SYLVIE. I'm ready.
MOLLY. We have to do this.
SYLVIE. I said I'm ready.
MOLLY. It's only a house. It's not a life.
SYLVIE. Fine.
MOLLY. Are you mad at me, Sylvie?
SYLVIE. No. I dunno. Maybe. Maybe I'm just sad.
MOLLY. It's just a house. It's not enough reason to stay.
SYLVIE. Were you and Daddy ever happy?
MOLLY. I can't remember.
SYLVIE. You were *never* happy?
MOLLY. I can't remember.
SYLVIE. Why did you have children?
MOLLY. We thought it would make us happy.
SYLVIE. Are you sorry you had us?

MOLLY. What are you saying, you? You and Roddy are the best things that ever happened in my life!

SYLVIE. (*Sobbing.*) Roddy, maybe. But, aren't you a little sorry you had me?

MOLLY. (*Moans.*) Oh, God, nooo, Sylvie! Don't ever think like that! I love you. I'm so glad that you're my daughter.

(MOLLY hugs SYLVIE, both weeping.)

MOLLY. Us girls have got to stick together.

(TAXI HORN honks, again, off. MOLLY looks up.)

MOLLY. Where is he? ... *Rodney!*

(RODDY (The YOUNGER) enters down staircase, carrying jacket and suitcase, ready to leave.)

RODDY. (THE YOUNGER) Here I am.
MOLLY. Are you ready?
RODDY. (THE YOUNGER) I'm ready.
MOLLY. Did you clean your room?
RODDY. (THE YOUNGER) I cleaned my room.
MOLLY. You made your bed?
RODDY. (THE YOUNGER) I made my bed.
MOLLY. (*To Sylvie.*) You made *your* bed?
SYLVIE. I made my bed.
MOLLY. Listen to me, children ... I don't know much, but, I know something. Here's the thing: You can

never be what you just were, two seconds ago. Things have
got to keep changing. This is Life. And me, I say "Thank
God for this!"

*(MOLLY and SYLVIE exit the house. RODDY pauses at
door, sets down his suitcase, turns, speaks to audience.
LIGHTS DIM in KITCHEN to SPOTLIGHT on
RODDY.)*

RODDY. (THE YOUNGER) I went to visit my
father, a couple of days later. He was staying at his
cousin's house in Woburn.

*(A SPOTLIGHT FADES UP on RODDY (The ELDER),
now playing ARCHIE, alone, downstage, sitting on
chair, looking out of imagined window. RODDY (The
YOUNGER) goes to him.)*

RODDY. (THE YOUNGER) Hi, Daddy.
ARCHIE. You're alone?
RODDY. (THE YOUNGER) Yes, sir.
ARCHIE. You know where your mother is?
RODDY. (THE YOUNGER) *(After a pause.)* Yes, sir.
I do.
ARCHIE. You're not going to tell me?
RODDY. (THE YOUNGER) No, sir.
ARCHIE. You scared of me, Roddy?
RODDY. (THE YOUNGER) Yes, sir. A little.

ARCHIE. Don't be. I used ta be scared of my father, too. You saw what my father was like, when he got old, yes? In the end, there's nothing to be scared of, believe me.

RODDY. (THE YOUNGER) I'm going to stay on living with Mama.

ARCHIE. You're what?

RODDY. (THE YOUNGER) I'm, uh, staying on living in with Mama.

ARCHIE. Why?

RODDY. (THE YOUNGER) Because I want to.

ARCHIE. Why?

RODDY. (THE YOUNGER) Because it's what I want to do.

ARCHIE. Did she poison you against me?

RODDY. (THE YOUNGER) No, sir. She didn't say anything, either way. I decided this myself.

ARCHIE. It's probably better. If you stick with me, the way I stuck with my father, you'll end up ...

(ARCHIE stops, mid-sentence. sobs. RODDY speaks to audience.)

RODDY. (THE YOUNGER) My father never finished his thought. He never told me how, exactly, I might have ended up, if he hadn't done what he was about to do ... if he hadn't reached out and cured me of the family disease, once and for all. (*Beat.*) I'll never know if my father planned it, or whether it was an accidental gift, but, in one split second of unexpected tenderness, my father changed my life and the lives of generations to follow ... He set us free.

(Suddenly, ARCHIE moans, in deep despair.)

ARCHIE. Somebody's got to stop me, Roddy! I'm a crazy person! I can't help myself!

(ARCHIE continues to sob. RODDY watches his father, awhile. sadly. Then, the BOY moves to his father, touches Archie's shoulder. Without warning, ARCHIE backhands his son, violently. The SOUND OF THE SLAP is amplified in the auditorium. It echoes, reverberates. RODDY flies backwards, stunned; hurt. ARCHIE sobs, again. There is a substantial pause in which the BOY will realize that he is free.)

RODDY. (THE YOUNGER) Thank you, sir. I ... I'm going.

(RODDY returns to staircase; faces audience, completes his contest speech. His voice is amplified.)

RODDY. (THE YOUNGER) I want to close by telling you the story of a friend of mine who had to conquer a lot of fear. My friend lived in a little town with his mother and his father and his sister. He wasn't very happy, but, he wasn't too unhappy, either. Most of the men in my friend's family were a little crazy. They didn't trust women very much. They always thought women were doing bad things. One day my friend's father hit my friend's mother ... really beat her up. My friend's mother and father got divorced and my friend had to go to court and decide whether he wanted to live with his mother and his sister, which meant he'd have to move away from his little town, or stay and live with his father. My friend was frightened to leave his town, and his school, and his friends ... He really wanted everything to just stay the way it always was, but, that wasn't possible. So, my friend thought about everything for a long, long time, and, finally, he thought about what Roosevelt said "We have nothing to fear but fear itself," and my friend thought that Roosevelt was really right, after all: Fear itself was probably the thing we have to be frightened of the most! ... Even though Roosevelt wasn't the great man everybody thought he was, he had figured something out about life, and people could, regardless of his faults, learn a lot from him. My friend found his courage. He chose to live with his mother and move away. I'm telling you this story, because, I, too, have learned a lot from Franklin Delano Roosevelt, and I also learned a lot from working on this speech. I learned how to think about things ... I learned how to stand up in front of people ... and speak my thoughts. For this opportunity, I want to thank the Red Feather Oratory Contest organizers, and I want to thank you: the audience. Thank you.

(LIGHTS CROSSFADE to RODDY (The ELDER), standing downstage. HE speaks directly to audience.)

RODDY. (THE ELDER) My mother found her dignity and she was *heroic*! She and my sister and I moved in with my mother's cousins. After a couple of months, we moved into our own apartment. It wasn't a beautiful place, but, it was partly furnished ... with a piano.

(LIGHT FADES UP ON MOLLY at piano, playing Chopin nocturne.)

RODDY. (THE ELDER) My mother learned to play Chopin and Bach and Brahms. We woke every morning to her playing, and fell asleep every night, same way. Our house was full of music. My mother never married again. She said "One marriage was enough." Sylvie never married, either. She moved to New York City, where she does something important in publishing. (*Pauses.*) My father stayed alone for the rest of his life. He always blamed my mother for his profound unhappiness. I called him just about once a month, on the phone, but, I never saw him, again, not face to face, until he died. (*Pauses; smiles.*) Me? I got married, had a bunch of kids ... one boy, three girls ... all of them lovely. My wife is brilliant and strong and beautiful, and I'm almost always proud of her, even though I'm also almost always jealous of other men staring at her beauty as they do. (*Smiles.*) I don't know much about people, really, but, I do know this, about myself: When the pressure's on me, my first thought is always to roar like a lion. But, I try to stop myself. Mostly, I do.

*(LIGHT FADES UP on RODDY (the YOUNGER),
outside house, staring in through upstage window,
coldly, grimly, suspiciously ... exactly as ARCHIE did,
in earlier scenes. But, then, the BOY smiles at Roddy
(the Elder) ... waves to him, happily. RODDY (the
ELDER) smiles, waves back. LIGHT FADES OUT.)*

RODDY. (THE ELDER) *(To audience.)* My son's a
lot like me, only nicer. He never roars at all.

*(Now, RODDY (the YOUNGER) enters house, goes to
Molly, takes Molly's hand. MOLLY stops playing
piano, rises from piano bench.*
*NOTE: MUSIC CONTINUES without interruption, on
tape, over sound system in auditorium.*
*RODDY (the YOUNGER) and his MOTHER dance to the
music.*
*RODDY (the ELDER) watches them dance for a few
moments, happily, before speaking the final words that
will end the play.)*

RODDY. (THE ELDER) *(To audience, directly.)* Like
my mother used to say: "Things have got to keep
changing! This is Life." ... And me, I say "Thank God for
this!"

*(ALL LIGHTS FADE OUT, but for LIGHT on MOLLY
and her SON, dancing. And then, after a moment,
THAT LIGHT FADES OUT, as well.)*

THE PLAY IS OVER

PROPERTIES LIST

Service for 5 including coffee cups and saucers
Silverware for 6
6 juice glasses
3 milk glasses
Coffee Pot w/ coffee
Large coffee mug for Archie
2 Frying Pan
Scrambled Eggs
Home Fries
Butter
Pitcher of Orange Juice
Bottle of Milk
Toaster with toast (practical)
Breakfast tray
Thermos
6 Cloth Napkins
Chopin Sheet Music
Cushion for Jacob's chair
Newspaper circa 1950
2 Bookbags for Roddy & Sylvie
Clipboard with Paperwork for Archie
Red sock
Green sock
Dish towels
Pot holders
Wastebasket
Bread knife
3 stools for truck

2 suitcases
1 child suitcase
Tea kettle
Tea bags
Broom
Dust pan
Pot scrubber

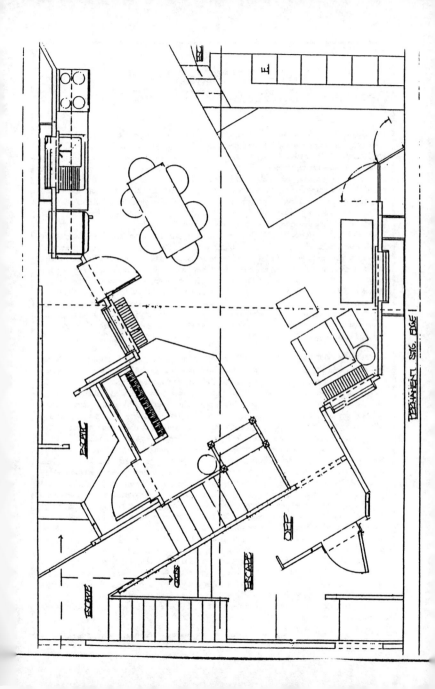

NEW COMEDIES FROM
SAMUEL FRENCH, INC.

MAIDS OF HONOR. (Little Theatre.) Comedy. Joan Casademont. 3m., 4f. Comb Int./Ext. Elizabeth McGovern, Laila Robins and Kyra Sedgwick starred in this warm, wacky comedy at Off-Broadway's famed WPA Theatre. Monica Bowlin, a local TV talk-show host, is getting married. Her two sisters, Isabelle and Annie, are intent on talking her out of it. It seems that Mr. Wonderful, the groom-to-be, is about to be indicted for insider trading, a little secret he has failed to share with his fiancee, Monica. She has a secret she has kept herself, too—she's pregnant, possibly not by her groom-to-be! All this is uncovered by delightfully kookie Isabelle, who aspires to be an investigative reporter. She'd also like to get Monica to realize that she is marrying the wrong man, for the wrong reason. She should be marrying ex-boyfriend Roger Dowling, who has come back to return a diary Monica left behind. And sister Annie should be marrying the caterer for the wedding, old flame Harry Hobson—but for some reason she can't relax enough to see how perfect he is for her. The reason for all three Bowlin women's difficulties with men, the reason why they have always made the wrong choice and failed to see the right one, is that they are the adult children of an alcoholic father and an abused mother, both now passed away, and they cannot allow themselves to love because they themselves feel unlovable. Sound gloomy and depressing? No, indeed. This delightful, wise and warm-hearted new play is loaded with laughs. We would also like to point out to all you actors that the play is also loaded with excellent monologues, at least one of which was recently included in an anthology of monologues from the best new plays.)   (#14961)

GROTESQUE LOVESONGS. (Little Theatre.) Comedy. Don Nigro. (Author of *The Curate Shakespeare As You Like It, Seascape with Sharks and Dancer* and other plays). This quirky new comedy about a family in Terre Haute, Indiana, enchanted audiences at NYC's famed WPA Theatre. Two brothers, Pete and John, live with their parents in a big old house with an attached greenhouse. The father, Dan, has a horticulture business. A pretty young woman named Romy is more or less engaged to marry younger brother Johnny as the play begins, and their prospects look quite rosy, for Johnny has just inherited a ton of money from recently-deceased family friend, Mr. Agajanian. Why, wonders Pete, has Agajanian left his entire estate to Johnny? He starts to persistently ask this question to his mother, Louise. Eventually, Louise does admit that, in fact, Mr. Agajanian was Johnny's father. This news stuns Johnny; but he's not *really* staggered until he goes down to the greenhouse and finds Pete and Romy making love. Pete, it seems, has always desperately wanted Romy; but when she chose Johnny instead he married a woman in the circus who turned out to be a con artist, taking him for everything he had and then disappearing. It seems everyone but Johnny is haunted by a traumatic past experience: Louise by her affair with Agajanian; Dan by the memory of his first true love, a Terre Haute whore; Pete by his failed marriage, and Romy by her *two* failed marriages. (One husband she left; the other was run over by a truckload of chickens [He loved cartoons so much, says Romy, that it was only fitting he should die like Wile E. Coyote.]). And, each character but Johnny knows what he wants. Louise and Dan want the contentment of their marriage; Romy wants to bake bread in a big old house—and she wants Pete, who finally admits that he wants her, too. And, finally, Johnny realizes what he wants. He does not want the money, or Agajanian's house. He wants to go to Nashville to make his own way as a singer of sad—yes, grotesque—love songs in the night. NOTE: this play is a treasure-trove of scene and monologue material.)   (#9925)